Minnow**Knits**

Uncommon Clothes to Knit for Kids

Jil Eaton

Lark Books

Editor: Carol Taylor
Technical writing and editing: Carla Patrick Scott
Copy editing: Julie Brown
Design and production: Elaine Thompson
Photography: Nina Fuller Carter
Photo styling: Merle Hagelin, Isabel Smiles, Chris Cantwell, and Jil Eaton
Illustrations: Jil Eaton

Library of Congress Cataloging-in-Publication Data
Eaton, Jil.
  Minnowknits : uncommon clothes to knit for kids / by Jil Eaton.
   p. cm.
  Includes bibliographical references and index.
  ISBN 0-887374-09-4
  1. Knitting--Patterns. 2. Children's clothing. I. Title.
 TT825.E28 1996
 746.43'20432--dc20   95-24990
                CIP

10 9 8 7 6 5 4 3 2

Published by Lark Books
50 College Street
Asheville, North Carolina, 28801, USA

© 1996, Jil Eaton

Distributed in Canada by Sterling Publishing,
  c/o Canadian Manda Group, One Atlantic Ave., Suite 105, Toronto,
  Ontario, Canada M6K 3E7
Distributed in Great Britain and Europe by Cassell PLC, Wellington House,
  125 Strand, London, England WC2R 0BB
Distributed in Australia by Capricorn Link (Australia) Pty Ltd., P.O.Box 6651,
  Baulkham Hills Business Centre, NSW, Australia 2153

ISBN 0-887374-09-4

MinnowKnits

DEDICATION

This book is dedicated to my mother, Nancy Whipple Lord, who taught me to knit when I was four; to my grandmother, Flora Hall Whipple, who taught my mother to knit; and to my son, Alexander Lord Eaton, who was the inspiration behind all the kids' stuff!

Contents

INTRODUCTION

Instructions for these hats are found on page 21.

It's magic: two sticks and a string, and you have a garment, an original creation, art to wear, a gift of love. There is an extraordinary, wonderful feeling that envelops you when you have a new knitting project, beautiful natural yarns in glorious colors, and the luxury of time to knit.

Knitting has been a constant delight throughout my life, ever since I learned to knit at the age of four. Maine winters are cold and long, and beginning in the crisp autumn afternoons in our big Victorian house, my mother and I would snuggle up by the fireside for a nap, our heads at opposite ends of our huge down couch, cozy under a hand-knitted afghan. Later, after cocoa, ginger cookies, and apples, the knitting would begin.

Recently, my mother found a trunk full of my earliest creations: rather oddly colorful outfits with big stitches and quite a few holes (but greatly original, nonetheless). Full-legged pantaloons outfitted most of my dolls and stuffed animals. Coats, hats, mittens, even dresses were attempted, some with more success than others, but all a bit offbeat, all expressing a sense of fun and a love of knitting.

Now, as a professional designer of hand-knitting patterns for children's wear, I still love fresh, unusual colorways and a bit of flair. (And I still include pantaloons in my collections!) The 24 projects in this book, including 37 individual patterns, present classic and traditional designs with a new twist, as well as chic and modern designs with clean, fresh silhouettes.

Yarns for the projects range from light, cool cottons to warm, washable wools, always in a gauge larger than generally specified for children's wear. The projects knit up quickly and easily, to the delight of knitters and their eager children alike. The patterns are sized from three months to eight years, based on the international sizing format, and the silhouettes are generous and comfortable for children to wear. (Please do check the measurements carefully when deciding what size to knit, and always check your gauge.)

As you rush headlong through your busy days, cherish the time you put aside for creating your wonderful hand-knits. I hope you will enjoy this little knitting smorgasbord as much as I enjoyed designing it, and that this book will get your creative energies going and your needles flying.

I also hope that you're teaching your daughters, sons, and friends to knit. Remember, when we are knitting, all is right with the world!

Jil Eaton

BAMBINIS

Bambinis, bébés, oh, babies! We love our babies, and what fun it is to knit for them. The patterns that follow are generous in both gauge and needle size—a great help to busy knitters. You'll even finish your project before the child is in college! Babies look sensational in bright and unusual colors, so be as zany as you like when you shop for yarn!

Baby Brit Sailor

Sizes

To fit 6-9 months
(1 year, 2 years)

Finished chest
20 (22, 24)"
<50.5 (56, 61) cm>

Length, shoulder to hem
8.5 (8.5, 9.5)"
<21.5 (21.5, 24) cm>

Materials

Worsted weight cotton that will
obtain gauge given below

For Sweater:

150 (175, 200) yards
<135 (158, 180) meters>
each color A and color B

For Hat:

65 (78, 93) yards <58 (70, 84)
meters> color A

25 (30, 40) yards <22 (27, 36)
meters> color B

25 yards <22 meters> red for
pom-poms

Knitting needles, one pair
straight and one set (4) double
pointed needles (dpn) size 8 US
(5 UK, 5.5mm) *or size needed
to obtain gauge.*

Gauge

18 sts and 24 rows = 4"
<10cm> in Stockinette st

*Always check gauge to save time
and ensure correct yardage!*

This hat and sweater make a bold statement in worsted weight cotton; they also work well in washable wool. The hat is made on two needles, so it's a zip to knit. Be prepared to be stopped on the street with this little attention getter!

SWEATER

Back

With color A, cast on 44 (48, 54) sts. Work in St st (k on RS, p on WS) for 7 rows. P 2 rows for turning ridge. Cont in St st for 10 (10, 9) rows. Then work in stripes as foll: *With color B, work 6 (6, 7) rows. With color A, work 6 (6, 7) rows. Rep from * for stripes for 52 (52, 58) rows. Neck: Work 12 (12, 14) sts and place on a holder for later finishing, attach 2nd ball of yarn and bind off middle 20 (24, 26) sts, work to end for left shoulder. Cont on left shoulder sts only with color B for 6 rows. Bind off.

Front

Work as for back until 3 rows less than back to shoulder. On next WS row, work to last 12 (12, 14) left shoulder sts, p1, (p2 tog, yo, p2) twice, yo, p2 tog, p1 (1, 2). Work 2 rows even. Bind off left shoulder sts, bind off 20 (24, 26) sts for neck. Place 12 (12, 14) right shoulder sts on holder for later finishing.

Sleeves

With *wrong sides facing*, place sts for both right shoulders on two parallel size 8 needles. With a third size 8 needle, k through first st on each needle, then the 2nd, and pass first over 2nd to bind off. Cont in this way to end for a knitted seam. Tack 1 st of front and back tog at right shoulder edge. With RS facing, mark for sleeves 6.25 (6.25, 7.25)" <16 (16, 18.5) cm> down from shoulder seam. With RS facing and B, pick up and k 56 (56, 66) sts between markers. Work in St st and stripe pat as back, dec 1 st each end every 3rd row 12 (12, 15) times, to 32 (32, 36) sts. Work even until 7 stripes have been worked. K 2 rows for folding ridge. Work in St st for 5 rows. Bind off loosely.

Finishing

Weave in all loose ends. Hem cuffs loosely. Sew sleeve and side seams. Sew buttons to button flap on left shoulder. Fold bottom hem inside and tack loosely.

HAT

With A, cast on 70 (80, 90) sts. Work in St st for 7 rows. P 2 rows for turning ridge. Cont in St st for 10 rows. Then work stripes as foll: (6 (7, 8) rows B, 6 (7, 8) rows A) twice. Divide sts in half on two size 8 needles. K sts tog as shoulders on sweater.

Finishing

Sew side seam. Fold bottom hem under and hem loosely. Attach two pom-poms to each point.

Pom-poms

Wind yarn around a 2" <5cm> strip of cardboard. Remove yarn from cardboard and tie around center with 8" <20cm> strand. Cut top and bottom loops and shake briskly. Use strands from center to sew to hat.

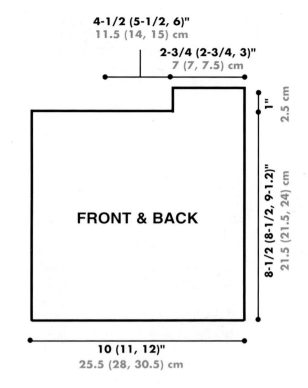

4-1/2 (5-1/2, 6)"
11.5 (14, 15) cm

2-3/4 (2-3/4, 3)"
7 (7, 7.5) cm

1"
2.5 cm

FRONT & BACK

8-1/2 (8-1/2, 9-1.2)"
21.5 (21.5, 24) cm

10 (11, 12)"
25.5 (28, 30.5) cm

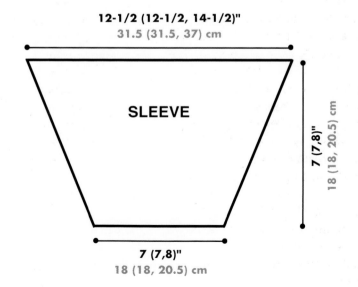

12-1/2 (12-1/2, 14-1/2)"
31.5 (31.5, 37) cm

SLEEVE

7 (7,8)"
18 (18, 20.5) cm

7 (7,8)"
18 (18, 20.5) cm

Tangerina

Sizes

6 months
(1 year, 2 years, 3 years)

Finished waist
20 (22, 23, 24)"
<51 (56, 58.5, 61) cm>

Materials

DK weight cotton that will
obtain gauge given below

360 (450, 500, 550) yards
<325 (410, 450, 500) meters>
color A

140 (180, 200, 220) yards
<126 (162, 180, 200) meters>
color B

100 yards <90 meters> color C

Knitting needles size 5 US (UK 8
4mm) *or size needed to obtain
gauge*

Size F US (8 UK, 4mm) crochet
hook

Four .75" <2cm> buttons

Gauge

22 sts and 28 rows = 4"
<10cm> over Stockinette stitch

*Always check gauge to save time
and ensure correct yardage!*

Color blocking is a great way to introduce several colors into a garment without carrying a tangle of multi-colored yarns across the back of the work. Many knitters have great success with this romper—perfect baby wear on bright spring and summer days at the park!

Pant Legs (make 2)

Cuff

With B, cast on 48 (64, 72, 80) sts. Work 4 rows even in Garter st, k all rows. Beg triangle pat on RS, using chart for 5 rows. P next row on WS. Work 4 rows Garter st with B.

Leg

On RS, with A, k and inc 66 (62, 60, 58) sts evenly across row. Work even on 114 (126, 132, 138) sts foll chart for pat st until piece measures 3.5 (4.5, 5, 6)" <9 (11.5, 12.5, 15) cm> above cuff.

Crotch Shaping

Beg RS, bind off 3 sts beg next 2 rows. Dec 1 st each end every other row 3 times to 102 (114, 120, 126) sts. With RS facing, sl sts for one leg on circular needle, place marker for center back, and sl sts of other leg to circular needle. Work even on 204 (228, 240, 252) sts until piece measures 11 (12.5, 13, 14)" <28 (31.5, 33, 36) cm> above cuff. K next rnd, dec 92 (106, 114, 120) sts evenly around to 112 (122, 126, 132) sts.

Bodice

Divide for front and back: Sl first 28 (30, 31, 33) sts and last 28 (31, 32, 33) sts to straight needle, place rem 56 (61, 63, 66) sts on holder for front. With C, cont on back sts as foll: Working back and forth in St st, work even for 14 rows, then, for armhole, bind off 3 sts at beg of next 2 rows, then dec 1 st each end every other row 3 times to 44 (49, 51, 54) sts. Work even until bodice measures 5 (6.75, 7.5, 8.25)" <12.5 (17, 19, 21) cm> from dividing row.

Neck shaping

Work 12 (14, 15, 15) sts, join 2nd skein and bind off center 20 (21, 21, 24) sts, work to end. Working both sides at same time, dec 1 st at neck edge every other row 3 times, 9 (11, 12, 12) sts rem for straps.

Buttonhole flaps

Begin Garter st, k each row, and dec 1 st each end every other row until 1 (1, 2, 2) sts rem., AT THE SAME TIME, after 4 rows, work buttonhole in center by k2 tog, yo. Pull yarn through rem sts.

Front

Sl sts from holder to straight needle. Join B and work back and forth in St st for 10 rows. Work buttonhole in 4th and 5th st from each edge by k2 tog, yo. Cont as for back, including armhole shaping, to 3 (4.25, 5.25, 6.25)" <7.5 (10.5, 13.5, 16) cm> from dividing row.

Neck shaping

Work 15 (17, 18, 18) sts, join 2nd skein and bind off center 14 (15, 15, 18) sts, work to end. Dec 1 st at neck edge every other row 6 times. Button flaps: Cont sts in Garter st for 1" <2.5cm>. Bind off.

Pockets

Picked-up patch pockets: With B, and a crochet hook, pick up the middle 33 sts on the pant leg, 6.5" <16.25 cm> down from dividing row and sl sts to needle. Work in St st for 4" <10cm>. Work triangle pat from chart for 5 rows. Bind off *firmly* with C. Sew pocket sides to pant leg.

Finishing

Weave in all loose ends. Single crochet around neck and bodice edges with matching colors. Sew buttons on front straps and back waist.

Stitch Pat

12

6-st rep

1

Triangle Pat

5

8-st rep

1

☐ k on RS, p on WS with A
⊟ p on RS, k on WS with A
⊡ k on RS, p on WS with B
⊠ k on RS, p on WS with C

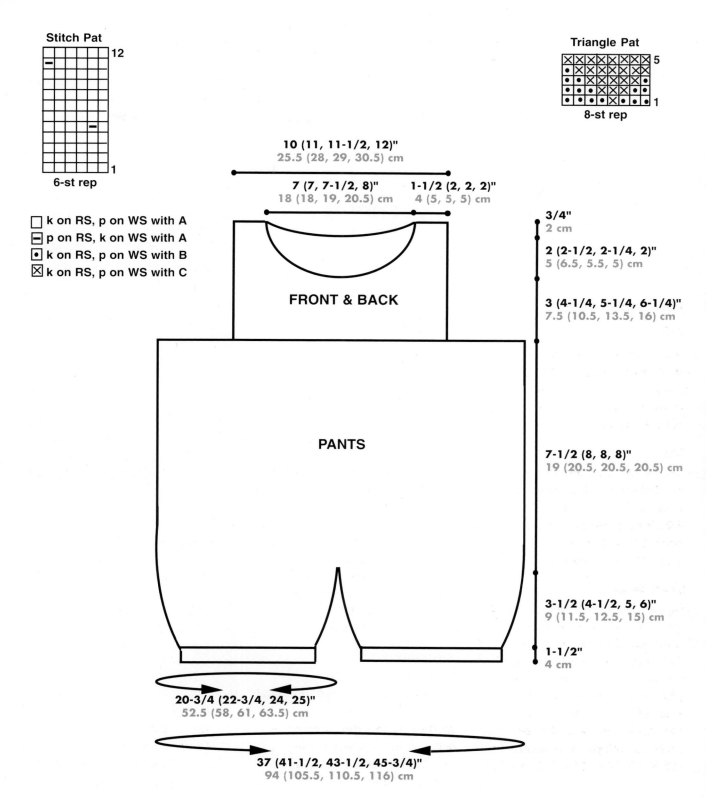

10 (11, 11-1/2, 12)"
25.5 (28, 29, 30.5) cm

7 (7, 7-1/2, 8)"
18 (18, 19, 20.5) cm

1-1/2 (2, 2, 2)"
4 (5, 5, 5) cm

3/4"
2 cm

2 (2-1/2, 2-1/4, 2)"
5 (6.5, 5.5, 5) cm

3 (4-1/4, 5-1/4, 6-1/4)"
7.5 (10.5, 13.5, 16) cm

FRONT & BACK

PANTS

7-1/2 (8, 8, 8)"
19 (20.5, 20.5, 20.5) cm

3-1/2 (4-1/2, 5, 6)"
9 (11.5, 12.5, 15) cm

1-1/2"
4 cm

20-3/4 (22-3/4, 24, 25)"
52.5 (58, 61, 63.5) cm

37 (41-1/2, 43-1/2, 45-3/4)"
94 (105.5, 110.5, 116) cm

Bon Bons

Sizes

To fit 6 months (1 year, 2 years, 4 years)

Finished Circumference:
15.5 (16, 16.5, 18)"
<39.5 (40.5, 42, 45.5) cm>

Materials

DK weight cotton that will obtain gauge given below

100 (135, 170, 200) yards <90 (122, 154, 180) meters> color A

50 yards <45 meters> each color B and color C

Knitting needles size 5 US (8 UK, 4mm) *or size needed to obtain gauge*

Gauge

22 sts and 28 rows = 4" <10cm> in Stockinette st.

Always check gauge to save time and to ensure correct yardage!

These cotton baby hats are wonderful for using up leftover yarn. You might also work the rolled band in a contrasting color, with delightful results. These hats are absolute show stoppers at baby showers!

Polka Dots

With size 5 needles and A, cast on 75 (80, 85, 90) sts. Work in St st (k on RS, p on WS) for 10 rows. K next row, inc 10 sts evenly across—85 (90, 95, 100) sts. P 1 row. (*Note:* Chart is drawn for size 1 year. For size 6 months, work 9 sts A between polka dots, for size 2 years work 11 sts A, and for size 4 years work 12 sts A.) Work in St st and chart pat for 22 rows. Cont with A only until piece measures 5 (5.75, 6.25, 6.5)" <12.5 (14.5, 16, 16.5) cm> from beg, dec 0 (2, 4, 1) sts on last row—85 (88, 91, 99) sts. Shape top and finish as for striped hat.

Stripes

Rolled bottom hem: With size 5 needles and A, cast on 75 (80, 83, 90) sts. Work in St st (k on RS, p on WS) for 10 rows. K next row, inc 10 (8, 8, 9) sts evenly across—85 (88, 91, 99) sts. P 1 row. Cont in St st and stripes as foll: *6 rows A, 4 rows B; rep from * once (once, twice, twice) more. Cont with A only until piece measures 5 (5.75, 6.25, 6.5)" <12.5 (14.5, 16, 16.5) cm> from beg, end with a WS row. Shape top—Next row (RS): *K2, k2 tog; rep from *, end k1 (0, 3, 3)—64 (66, 69, 75) sts. Work 1 row even. Next row: *K2, k2 tog; rep from *, end k0 (2, 1, 3)—48 (50, 52, 57) sts. Work 1 row even. Next row: *K2, k2 tog; rep from *, end k0 (2, 0, 1)—36 (38, 39, 43) sts. Work 1 row even. K2 tog across next row, end k0 (0, 1, 1)—18 (19, 20, 22) sts. P2 tog across next row.

Finishing

Cut yarn, leaving a long tail for sewing. Pull through rem sts and sew back seam, reversing seam on first 10 rows of St st for rolled edge. Make tassel by winding 15 yards <15 meters> C around a 3" <7.5cm> cardboard rectangle. Cut another yarn and tie through center for the tassel top. Tie a 2nd yarn around tassel 1" <2.5cm> from top. Cut bottom loops and trim evenly. Sew to top of hat so tassel stands up straight.

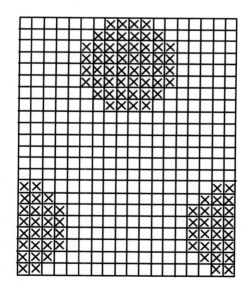

☐ = color A

☒ = color B

Surprise! Chapeau

Sizes

To fit 6 months (1 year, 2 years, 4 years)

Finished Circumference:
14.5 (15.5, 16.5, 18)"
<37 (39.5, 42, 45.5) cm>

Materials

DK weight wool/cotton blend and chenille that will obtain gauge given below

105 (110, 125, 135) yards <94 (100, 112, 122) meters> MC

20 (30, 40, 50) yards <18 (27, 36, 45) meters> CC

Knitting needles size 5 US (8 UK, 4mm) *or size needed to obtain gauge.*

Sample in photograph knit in Stahl Olé #S621 and Surprise Chenille #0604

Gauge

22 sts and 28 rows = 4" <10cm> in Stockinette st.

Always check gauge to save time and to ensure correct yardage!

You can make two very different hats with this pattern, depending on your yarns. If chenille is used for both the beehive ridges and the tassel, the hat is looser and more bubbly. Working the ridges in a single yarn and the tassel in chenille gives you a tighter cloche and a more delicate shape. Either way, you and your little one will get a bit of applause!

Stripe Pattern

Row 1 (WS): With CC, purl.

Rows 2 and 3: With CC, work in rev St st (p on RS, k on WS).

Rows 4-7: With MC, work in St st (k on RS, p on WS).

Row 8 (RS): With CC, knit.

Rows 9 and 10: With CC, work in rev St st.

Rows 11-14: With MC, work in St st.

Rep rows 1-14 for stripe pat.

Cap

With size 5 needles and MC, cast on 74 (80, 86, 92) sts. Work in St st for 10 rows. K next row, inc 6 sts evenly across—80 (86, 92, 98) sts. Work in stripe pat for 20 (20, 34, 34) rows. Next row (WS): With MC, *p4, p2 tog; rep from *, end p2—67 (72, 77, 82) sts. Work 6 rows in pat. Next Row (RS): With MC, *k3, k2 tog; rep from *, end k2—54 (58, 62, 66) sts. Work 7 rows in pat. Next Row: With MC, k2 tog across— 27 (29, 31, 33) sts. Next Row: With MC, p2 tog across, end p1—14 (15, 16, 17) sts. Next Row: With MC, k2 tog across—7 (8, 8, 9) sts.

Finishing

Cut yarn, leaving a long tail for sewing. Pull through rem sts and sew back seam, reversing seam at first 10 rows of St st for rolled edge. Make tassel by winding 15 yards <13 meters> MC around a 3" <7.5cm> card-board rectangle. Cut another yarn and tie through center for the tassel top. Tie a 2nd yarn around tassel 1" <2.5cm> from top. Cut bottom loops and trim evenly. Sew to top of hat so tassel stands up straight.

A second hat may be made using the same pattern and all DK weight yarn for the hat body and chenille for the tassel. The finished hat will have a snug, shorter fit.

Zany Bambini

Sizes

To fit 6 months (1 year, 2 years)

Finished chest:
19.5 (22, 25)"
<49.5 (56, 63.5) cm>

Length, shoulder to hem:
9 (10, 11.25)"
<23 (25.5, 28.5) cm>
(with lower edge rolled)

Materials

DK weight cotton that will
obtain gauge given at right

For Pullover and Hat:

400 (500, 600) yards <360
(450, 540) meters> MC

100 yards <90 meters> each
color A and color B

For Pantaloons:

200 (300, 400) yards <180 (270,
360) meters> MC, 100 yards <90
meters> each color A and color B

Knitting needles size 5 US
(8 UK, 4mm) *or size needed to
obtain gauge*, size 2 US (11 UK,
2.75mm) (for suspenders)

Size 5 circular needle 20"
<51cm> long (for pantaloons)

Three .5" <1.5cm> buttons (for
Pulllover); four .5" <1.5cm>
buttons (for Pantaloons)

Elastic for pantaloons waistband, 15 (16, 18)" <38 (40.5,
45.5) cm> long, 1" <2.5cm>
wide

Stitch holders and stitch markers

Cable needle (cn)

This hat-sweater-pantaloon ensemble was originally designed in orange, green, purple, and red colorways. Use your designer instincts and your own inspired colors. (Experiment with small swatches until you have the right balance.) Go ahead and be zany!

Gauge

22 sts and 36 rows = 4"
<10cm> in Seed st

Always check gauge to save time and ensure correct yardage!

Pattern Stitches

Seed St

Row 1 (RS): *K1, p1; rep from * to end.

Row 2: K the purl sts and p the knit sts. Rep row 2 for Seed st.

Cable Pat (over 10 sts)

Row 1 (RS): P2, k6, p2.

Row 2 and all WS rows through row 8: K2, p6, k2.

Row 3: P2, sl next 3 sts to cn and hold in back of work, k3, k3 from cn, p2.

Rows 5 and 7: Rep row 1.

Rep rows 1-8 for cable pat.

SWEATER

Back

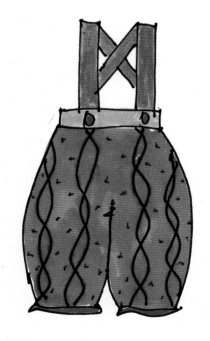

With size 5 needles and B, cast on 54 (62, 70) sts. Work in St st (k on RS, p on WS) for 10 rows. Join A and k 4 rows for Garter ridges. Join MC and k next row on RS, inc 8 sts evenly spaced across—62 (70, 78) sts. Beg pat: Next row (WS): Work 8 (10, 12) sts in Seed st, *k2, p6, k2 (10 sts cable pat), work 8 (10, 12) sts Seed st; rep from * twice more. Cont in pats as established for 8 (9, 10)" <20.5 (23, 25.5) cm> more. On next (RS) row, work 20 (23, 25) sts and place on a holder for right shoulder, work next 22 (24, 28) sts and place on a 2nd holder for back neck, work to end. Working on left shoulder sts only, k next row on WS for turning ridge. Cont in St st (k on RS, p on WS) for 6 rows for button placket. Bind off.

Front

Work as for back until 6.25 (7.25, 8)" <16 (18.5, 20.5) cm> above Garter ridge.

Neck shaping: Work 24 (28, 31) sts, join 2nd skein of yarn and bind off center 14 (14, 16) sts for neck, work to end. Working both sides at same time, dec 1 st at neck edge every other row 4 (5, 6) times—20 (23, 25) sts each side. Work even until piece measures 3 rows less than back to right shoulder. On next (WS) row, work button-holes on left front shoulder as foll: Work 0 (1, 1) st, p2 tog, yo, work 9 (9, 10) sts, p2 tog, yo, work 3 (4, 4) sts, p2 tog, yo, work to end. Work 2 rows even. Bind off left shoulder sts. Place right shoulder sts on a holder.

Sleeves

Slip shoulder sts from holder to two straight needles. *With WS tog* and a third straight needle, k the first st on front needle tog with first st on back needle, *k next st on front and back needles tog, sl the first st over 2nd st to bind off; rep from * until all sts are bound off. Fold turning ridge of left back shoulder to WS and tack side of placket along back shoulder edge, then tack 1 st of front and back tog at shoulder edge.

Place markers on front and back 4.5 (5.5, 6.5)" <11.5 (14, 16.5) cm> down from shoulder seams for armholes. With RS facing, larger needles, and A, pick up and k50 (60, 72) sts between markers. K 3 rows, inc 8 (10, 8) sts evenly across last row—58 (70, 80) sts. Beg pat: Next row (RS): Work 6 (10, 13) sts in Seed st, *10 sts cable pat, 8 (10, 12) sts Seed st; rep from * once more, 10 sts cable pat, 6 (10, 13) sts Seed st. Cont in pats as established for 3 rows more. Cont in pat, dec 1 st each end of next row, then every 12th (8th, 4th) row 5 (5, 2) times, then every 6th row 0 (4, 10) times—46 (50, 54) sts. Work even until sleeve measures 7.5 (8, 8.5)" <19 (20.5, 21.5) cm>. Join B and work in k1, p1 rib for 4 (4, 6) rows. Bind off in rib.

Finishing

Neckband: With RS facing, smaller needles, and A, beg at left front shoulder, pick up and k66 (70, 74) sts evenly around neck edge, including sts from holders. Work in St st (k on RS, p on WS) for 8 (12, 16) rows. K 2 rows. Bind off. Sew side and sleeve seams. Sew on buttons.

PANTALOONS

Legs (make 2)

With straight needles and A, cast on 59 (67, 75) sts. Work in St st (k on RS, p on WS) for 11 rows. Join MC and p next row on WS, inc 19 sts evenly spaced across—78 (86, 94) sts. Beg pat: Next row (RS): Work 12 (14, 16) sts in Seed st, *10 sts cable pat, 12 (14, 16) sts Seed st; rep from * twice more. Cont in pats as established until 5 (6.25, 7.5)" <12.5 (16, 19) cm> have been worked above St st.

Crotch shaping

Bind off 3 sts at beg of next 2 rows. Dec 1 st each end every other row 3 (4, 5) times—66 (72, 78) sts. With RS facing, join both legs on circular needle—132 (144, 156) sts. Join and place marker for beg of rnd. Cont to work pats in rnds until 10.25 (11.5, 13)" <26 (29, 33) cm> have been worked above St st. K next row on WS, working k2 tog around—66 (72, 78)

HAT

Color blocked, cabled hat with rolled hem and tassel.

Hem

With straight needles and A, cast on 80 (85, 90) sts. Work in St st for 11 rows. Join MC and p next row on WS, inc 10 sts evenly spaced across—90 (95, 100) sts.

Beg pat: Next row (RS): *Work 10 sts cable pat, 8 (9, 10) sts Seed st; rep from * to end. Cont in pats as established until 3.5 (4, 4.5)" <9 (10, 11.5) cm> have been worked above St st. Next row (RS): *Work 10 sts cable pat, k2 tog, work to 2 sts before next cable pat, k2 tog; rep from * to end. Work 1 row even. Rep last 2 rows until all Seed sts have been dec'd.

sts. Join B and cont in St st (k every rnd) for 8 rnds. P next rnd for turning ridge. K 7 rnds more. Place sts on a strand of yarn for later finishing.

Suspenders (make 2)

With size 2 needles and A, cast on 8 sts. K 3 rows. Cont in Seed st, working buttonhole on next row as foll: work 3 sts, yo, k2 tog, work to end. Cont in Seed st for 14 (16, 18)" <35.5 (40.5, 45.5) cm>. Make another buttonhole. K 3 rows. Bind off.

Finishing

Sew crotch and leg seams. Sew buttons to outside front over cable and inside back waistband. Place elastic under waistband and sew live sts to inside seam.

Finishing

Cut yarn, leaving an end for sewing. Pull through rem sts and sew back seam, reversing seam at lower edge for rolled hem. With A, make a tassel, winding yarn around a 3.5" <9cm> rectangle cardboard. Remove cardboard and pull through an 8" <20.5cm> strand of yarn. Tie another strand 1" <2.5cm> down from the top. Cut loops at other end and trim evenly. Sew to top of hat.

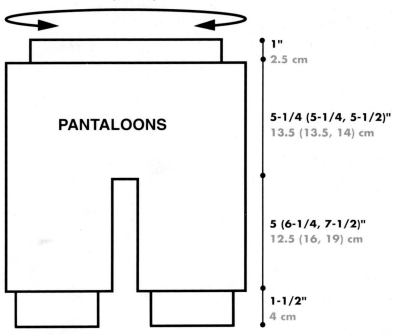

20-3/4 (22-1/2, 24-1/2)"
52.5 (57, 62) cm

PANTALOONS

1"
2.5 cm

5-1/4 (5-1/4, 5-1/2)"
13.5 (13.5, 14) cm

5 (6-1/4, 7-1/2)"
12.5 (16, 19) cm

1-1/2"
4 cm

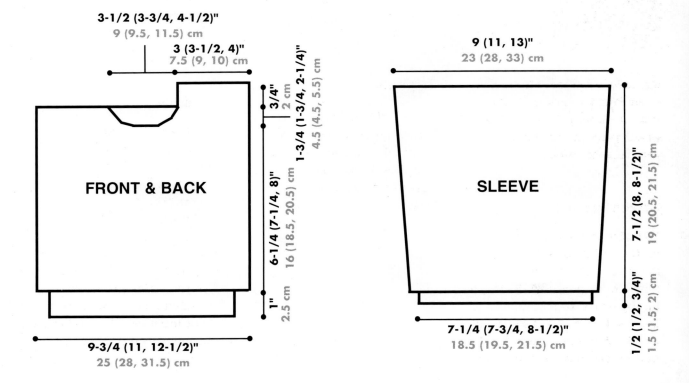

3-1/2 (3-3/4, 4-1/2)"
9 (9.5, 11.5) cm

3 (3-1/2, 4)"
7.5 (9, 10) cm

FRONT & BACK

3/4"
2 cm

1-3/4 (1-3/4, 2-1/4)"
4.5 (4.5, 5.5) cm

6-1/4 (7-1/4, 8)" 16 (18.5, 20.5) cm

1"
2.5 cm

9-3/4 (11, 12-1/2)"
25 (28, 31.5) cm

9 (11, 13)"
23 (28, 33) cm

SLEEVE

7-1/2 (8, 8-1/2)" 19 (20.5, 21.5) cm

1/2 (1/2, 3/4)" 1.5 (1.5, 2) cm

7-1/4 (7-3/4, 8-1/2)"
18.5 (19.5, 21.5) cm

Beau Jest

Sizes

3-6 months (1 year, 2 years, 3 years)

Finished waist:
17 (20, 21.5, 23)"
<43 (51, 54.5, 58.5) cm>

Materials

100% mercerized cotton that will obtain gauge given below

200 (270, 290, 320) yards <180 (245 260, 290) meters> color A

70 (70, 100, 120) yards <65 (65, 90, 108) meters> color B

70 (70, 70, 70) yards <65 (65, 65, 65) meters> each colors C and D

Knitting needles size 8 (UK 5, 5.5mm) *or size needed to obtain gauge.* Size 8 (UK 5, 5.5 mm) circular needle 36" <91.5cm> long, Size F (8 UK, 4 mm) crochet hook

Four 1" <2.5cm> buttons

Six .5" <1.5cm> button for crotch, if desired

Sample in photograph knit in Crystal Palace Montery, #34 Blue (A), #61 Red (B), #72 Green (C), and #57 White (D)

This color-blocked romper is made from a slightly heavier cotton, at 4.5 stitches to the inch (2.5 cm). The yarn makes a fabric with nice body, so the shape holds up well, no matter how much your baby romps! For warmer climates, try a lighter gauge cotton; just adjust your sizing accordingly— after making your gauge swatch, of course!

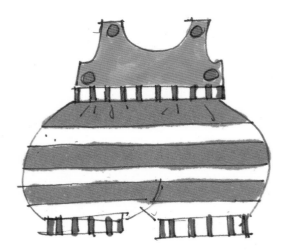

Gauge

16 sts and 24 rows = 4"
<10cm> over Stockinette st

*Always check gauge to save
time and ensure correct
yardage!*

Pant Legs Make two

Cuff

With C, cast on 48 (52, 56, 60)
sts. Work 6 rows in St st (k on
RS, p on WS). P 1 row on RS for
turning ridge. Add D and beg
vertical stripes as foll: *P2 sts C,
then 2 sts D, and repeat from *
across row. Cont in St st, in
stripe pat, for 1" <2.5cm> from
turning ridge.

Leg

Begin horizontal stripes, by
dropping C, and joining A and
inc 1 st in each st to 96 (104,

112, 120) sts. Work 12 (14, 14,
16) rows with A. Work 4 rows
D. Continue in St st, *alternating
horizontal stripes with A and D,*
until piece measures 2.5 (3, 3,
3.5)" <6.5 (7.5, 7.5, 9) cm>
above turning ridge. At the
same time, on RS, if desired,
make buttonholes for sizes 3-6
mo, 1 and 2 years beginning 1"
<2.5cm> from turning ridge,
and every 2" <5cm> by k2 from
RS edge, k2 tog, yo.

Crotch Shaping

On RS, bind off 3 sts at beg of
next 2 rows. Dec 1 st each end
every other row 3 times to 84
(92, 100, 108) sts, cont in
stripe pat. *With RS facing,* sl sts
for one leg onto circular needle,
place marker for center back,
and sl sts of other leg onto circular needle. Join and work
even on 168 (184, 200, 216)
sts until piece measures 8 (9,
9.5, 10.5)" <20.5 (23, 24, 26.5)

cm> above turning ridge, ending with 10 (12, 14, 16) rows A.
K2 tog on last rnd to 84 (92,
100, 108) sts.

Waistband

Drop A and add C, and work 1"
<2.5cm> vertical stripe pat with
C and D as for leg bottom.

Bodice

Divide for front and back: Sl
first 21 (23, 25, 27) sts and last
21 (23, 25, 27) sts to straight
needle, place rem 42 (46, 50,
54) sts on holder for front.

Back

Join B, and cont on back sts as
foll: Working back and forth in St
st, work even for 1" <2.5cm>.
For armholes, bind off 2 sts at
beg of next 2 rows, then dec 1
st each end every other row 3
times to 32 (36, 40, 44) sts.
Work even until bodice measures 2 (3.25, 4.25, 5.25)" <5 (8,
11, 13.5) cm> from dividing row.

Neck shaping

Work 9 (10, 11, 12) sts. Join
2nd skein and bind off middle
14 (16, 18, 20) sts, work to
end. *Working both sides at
same time,* dec 1 st at neck
edge every other row 3 times,
until straps have 6 (7, 8, 9) sts
remaining. Work even for 4
rows, and bind off firmly on RS.

Front

Sl sts from holder to straight

needle. Join B and work back and forth in St st as for back. After two rows, work buttonhole on RS in 2nd and 3rd st from each edge by k2 tog, yo. Cont as for back, including armhole and neck shaping. *Make shoulder strap buttonholes* as foll: On last neck dec, work buttonholes by k2 tog, yo in middle of row. Work 4 more rows and bind off firmly.

Finishing

Weave in all loose ends. Crochet a sl st around neck and bodice edges with B. Sew buttons on back shoulders, and back waist and crotch if necessary.

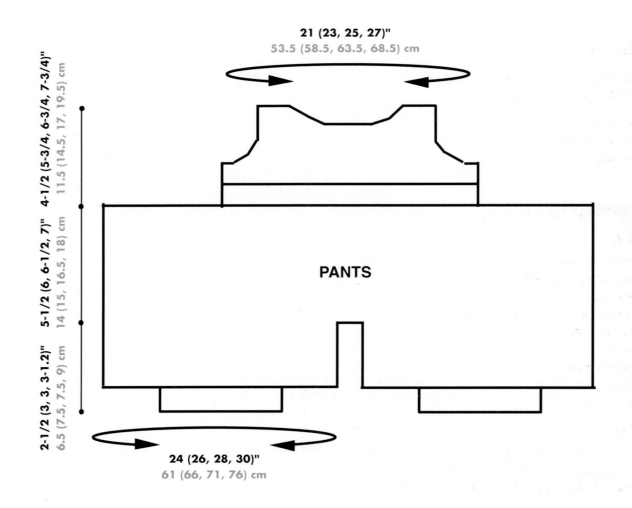

21 (23, 25, 27)"
53.5 (58.5, 63.5, 68.5) cm

4-1/2 (5-3/4, 6-3/4, 7-3/4)"
11.5 (14.5, 17, 19.5) cm

5-1/2 (6, 6-1/2, 7)"
14 (15, 16.5, 18) cm

2-1/2 (3, 3, 3-1.2)"
6.5 (7.5, 7.5, 9) cm

PANTS

24 (26, 28, 30)"
61 (66, 71, 76) cm

JUMPING BEANS

These outfits are the zaniest of the lot, color-bright and enchanting to knit and to wear. Simple enough even for beginning knitters, these charming antidotes to stuffiness poke fun at tradition. From stripes to polka dots, from cotton to mohair, let your imagination run wild, and knit up a batch of beans!

Polka Dots

Sizes

To fit 2 (4, 6, 8, 10) years

Finished chest:
27 (30, 32, 34, 36)"
<68.5 (76, 81, 86.5, 91.5) cm>

Length, shoulder to hem:
12 (14.5, 16.5, 18, 19.5)"
<30.5 (37, 42, 45.5, 49.5) cm>

Materials

Worsted weight cotton that will obtain gauge given below

135 (180, 220, 250, 285) yards
<120 (162, 198, 225, 256) meters> color A

120 (160, 190, 220, 250) yards
<108 (144, 170, 198, 225) meters> color B

70 (90, 110, 130, 150) yards
<63 (80, 100, 117, 135) meters> each colors C and D

50 (65, 80, 90, 110) yards
<45 (58, 72, 80, 100) meters> each colors E and F

Knitting needles sizes 4 and 6 US (9 and 7 UK, 3.5 and 4.5mm) or size needed to obtain gauge, size 6 double pointed needles (dpn). Size F US (8 UK, 4mm) crochet hook.

Stitch holders and markers

Sample in photograph knit in Rowan Cotton DK, #263 Bleached White (A), #241 Lettuce (B), #287 Diana (blue) (C), #234 Lime (D), #233 Cerise (E), and #249 Pimpernel (red orange) (F)

This pullover will delight even a fussy ten-year-old! The silhouette is simple, and the sweater is comfortable, as well as slightly off-beat.

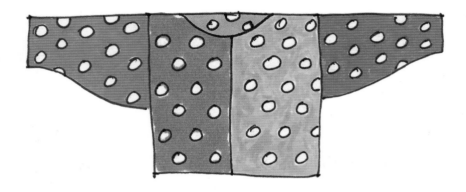

Gauge

20 sts and 28 rows = 4"
<10cm> over Stockinette st
using larger needles

*Always check gauge to save
time and ensure correct
yardage!*

Back

With smaller needles and B,
cast on 68 (76, 80, 86, 90) sts.
Work in k1, p1 rib for 1"
<2.5cm>. Change to larger nee-
dles. Establish polka dot pat—
Next row (RS): Beg with st 2 (3,
1, 3, 1) of chart, work to rep,
work 10-st rep 6 (7, 7, 8, 8)
times, work last 4 (3, 5, 3, 5)
sts of chart. Cont in pat as
established until piece measures 12 (14.5, 16.5, 18, 19.5)"
<30.5 (37, 42, 45.5, 49.5) cm>
from beg. Place 20 (24, 25, 28,
30) sts on a holder for one

shoulder, place next 28 (28, 30,
30, 30) sts on a 2nd holder for
back neck, place rem 20 (24,
25, 28, 30) sts on a 3rd holder
for other shoulder.

Front

With smaller needles, cast on
34 (38, 40, 43, 45) sts with D
for left front and 34 (38, 40,
43, 45) sts with C for right
front. Work as for back until
piece measures 10 (12.5, 14,
15.5, 17)" <25.5 (32, 35.5, 39,
43) cm> from beg. Work neck
shaping as foll: Next RS row,
work 34 (38, 40, 43, 45) sts,
with C, bind off next 6 (6, 7, 7,
7) sts, work to end. Next WS
row, work 28 (32, 33, 36, 38)
sts of right front, with D, bind
off next 6 (6, 7, 7) sts, work to
end. Working both sides at
same time, bind off from each
neck edge 3 sts once, 2 sts

once, 1 st 3 times. Work even
until same length as back. Place
rem 20 (24, 25, 28, 30) sts
each side on holders for later
finishing.

Sleeves

With *wrong sides facing*, place
sts for both right shoulders on
two parallel dpn. With a third
dpn, k through first st on each
needle, then the 2nd, and pass
first over 2nd to bind off. Cont
in this way to end for a knitted
seam. Work in same way for
left shoulder seam. With RS
facing, mark for sleeves 6.5 (7,
7.5, 8, 8.5)" <16.5 (18, 19,
20.5, 21.5) cm> down from
shoulder seam. With RS facing
and E for right sleeve, F for left
sleeve, pick up and k66 (70,
76, 80, 86) sts between markers. Establish polka dot pat—
Next row (WS): Beg with st 3
(1, 3, 1, 3), work to rep, work
10-st rep 6 (6, 7, 7, 8) times,
work last 3 (5, 3, 5, 3) sts of
chart. Cont in pat as established for 2 rows more, then
dec 1 st each end of next row,
then every 4th row 4 (13, 16,
19, 19) times more, then every
other row 12 (3, 2, 0, 3) times.
When sleeve measures 7 (9.5,
11, 12.5, 13)" <18 (24, 28, 32,
33) cm>, work 1" <2.5cm> in
k1, p1 rib with same color as
pick-up row on rem 32 (36, 38,
40, 40) sts. Bind off loosely
and evenly in rib.

Finishing

For neckband, with crochet hook and matching background color, work 1 rnd sc evenly around neck edge. Sew side and sleeve seams. Weave in all loose ends.

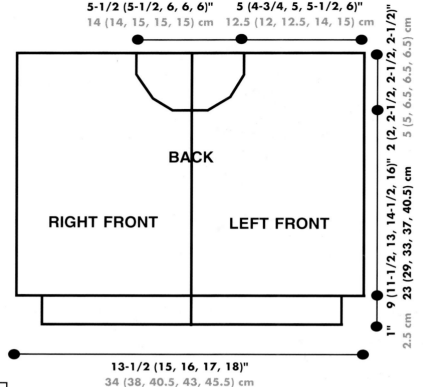

5-1/2 (5-1/2, 6, 6, 6)"
14 (14, 15, 15, 15) cm

5 (4-3/4, 5, 5-1/2, 6)"
12.5 (12, 12.5, 14, 15) cm

2 (2, 2-1/2, 2-1/2, 2-1/2)"
5 (5, 6.5, 6.5, 6.5) cm

9 (11-1/2, 13, 14-1/2, 16)"
23 (29, 33, 37, 40.5) cm

1"
2.5 cm

BACK

RIGHT FRONT

LEFT FRONT

13-1/2 (15, 16, 17, 18)"
34 (38, 40.5, 43, 45.5) cm

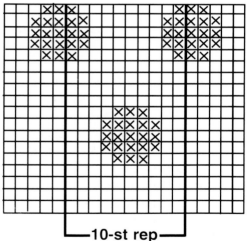

—10-st rep—

□ = color B for Back
   = color C for Right Front
   = color D for Left front
   = color E for Right Sleeve
   = color F for Left Sleeve

⊠ = color A

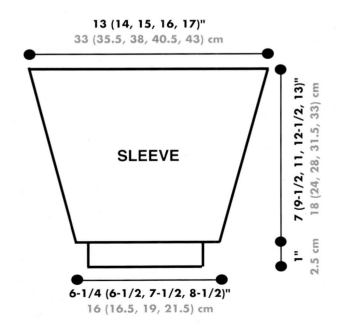

13 (14, 15, 16, 17)"
33 (35.5, 38, 40.5, 43) cm

SLEEVE

7 (9-1/2, 11, 12-1/2, 13)"
18 (24, 28, 31.5, 33) cm

1"
2.5 cm

6-1/4 (6-1/2, 7-1/2, 8-1/2)"
16 (16.5, 19, 21.5) cm

41

Gumdrops

Sizes

To fit 1 year (2 years, 4 years, 6 years)

Finished chest:
21 (22, 26, 30)"
<54 (56, 66, 76) cm>

Length, shoulder to hem:
11 (12, 15, 18)"
<28 (30.5, 38, 45.5) cm>

Materials

100% mohair or mohair blend that will obtain gauge given below

192 (215, 316, 410) yards <175 (195, 285, 370) meters> MC

Small amounts of contrasting colors Teal, Purple, Red/Orange, Lime for bobbles

Knitting needles size 9 US (4 UK, 6mm) *or size needed to obtain gauge*

Stitch holders

Crochet hook size G (7 UK, 4.50mm)

Sample in photograph knit in Classic Elite LaGran Mohair Hot Pink (MC)

Gauge

16 sts and 22 rows = 4" <10cm> over Stockinette st

Always check gauge to save time and ensure correct yardage!

Mohair is a light, strong, gorgeous yarn, a favorite for European children's wear. It's also one of my favorites— one of the easi- est and quickest to knit. The free- form placement of the multi- colored bobbles on this sweater gives you a little creative lift at the end!

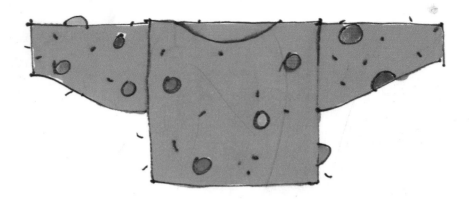

Back

With MC, cast on 38 (41, 47, 56) sts. Work k2, p1 rib for 2 (2, 2.5, 2.5)" <5 (5, 6.5, 6.5) cm>. On next RS row, k and inc 4 (3, 5, 4) sts evenly across row to 42 (44, 52, 60) sts. Cont in St st, (k on RS, p on WS), until piece measures 8.5 (9.5, 12.5, 15.5)" <22 (24, 32, 40) cm> from beg.

Neck

Work 14 (14, 17, 20) sts, attach 2nd ball of yarn and bind off middle 14 (16, 18, 20) sts, work to end. *Working both sides at same time,* dec 1 st at each neck edge every other row 4 times. Work even until piece measures 11 (12, 15, 18)" <28 (30.5, 38, 45.5) cm> from beg. Place 10 (10, 13, 16) shoulder sts on holders for later finishing.

Front

Work as for back.

Sleeves

With *wrong sides facing,* place sts for both right shoulders on two parallel size 9 needles. With a third size 9 needle, k through first st on each needle, then the 2nd, and pass first over 2nd to bind off. Cont in this way to end for a knitted seam. With RS facing, mark for sleeves 5.5 (6, 6.5, 7.5)" <14 (15, 16.5, 19) cm> down from shoulder seam. With RS facing and MC, pick up and k44 (48, 52, 60) sts between markers. Work in St st for 4 rows. Cont in St st, dec 1 st each end of next row, then every 4th row 5 (4, 3, 4) times more, every other row 5 (7, 10, 11) times to 22 (24, 24, 28) sts. Work even until sleeve measures 6 (6.5, 7, 8)" <15 (16.5, 18, 20) cm>. P 1 row for turning ridge. Work in St st for 1 (1, 1.5, 1.5)" <2.5 (2.5, 4, 4) cm>. Bind off loosely.

Bobbles

Cast on 1 st and make 5 in 1 st bobbles as foll: (Knit the st in the front loop, then in the back loop keeping it on the left needle) twice, knit in the front loop once more, turn, p5, turn, k5, turn, p5, turn. Pass the 2nd, 3rd, 4th and 5th sts over the first st. Cut and pull tail through for sewing.

Finishing

Weave in all loose ends. Make bobbles in various colors, and sew on randomly as desired. Single crochet around neckline with MC. Sew sleeve and side seams. Loosely hem cuffs to inside sleeves.

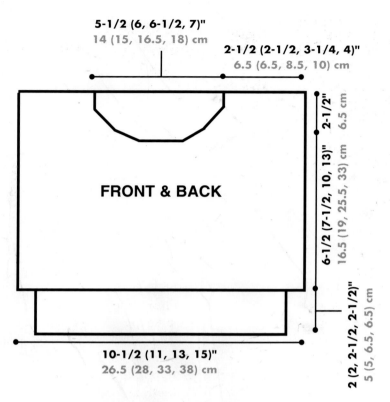

5-1/2 (6, 6-1/2, 7)"
14 (15, 16.5, 18) cm

2-1/2 (2-1/2, 3-1/4, 4)"
6.5 (6.5, 8.5, 10) cm

FRONT & BACK

2-1/2"
6.5 cm

6-1/2 (7-1/2, 10, 13)"
16.5 (19, 25.5, 33) cm

2 (2, 2-1/2, 2-1/2)"
5 (5, 6.5, 6.5) cm

10-1/2 (11, 13, 15)"
26.5 (28, 33, 38) cm

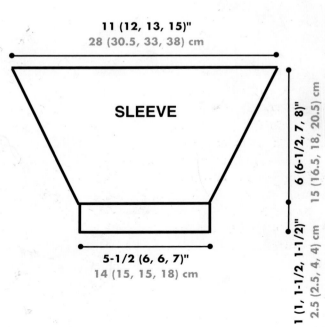

11 (12, 13, 15)"
28 (30.5, 33, 38) cm

SLEEVE

6 (6-1/2, 7, 8)"
15 (16.5, 18, 20.5) cm

1 (1, 1-1/2, 1-1/2)"
2.5 (2.5, 4, 4) cm

5-1/2 (6, 6, 7)"
14 (15, 15, 18) cm

Coco Chenille

Sizes

To fit 6 months (1 year, 2 years, 3 years, 4 years)

Finished chest, sweater:
19.5 (22, 25, 27, 29)"
<49.5 (56, 63.5, 68.5, 73.5) cm>

Length, shoulder to hem:
9 (10, 12, 13, 14)"
<23 (25.5, 30.5, 33, 35.5) cm>

Materials

Worsted weight chenille that will obtain gauge given below

395 (475, 590, 680, 800) yards <354 (428, 530, 612, 720) meters> MC

70 (80, 90, 110, 120) yards <64 (72, 82, 100, 108) meters> CC

Knitting needles size 6 US (7 UK, 4.5mm). Size 6 circular needle 16 or 24" <40 or 60 cm> long. Double pointed needles (dpn), size 6 or *size needed to obtain gauge*

Stitch holders and markers

Two .5" <1.5cm> buttons

1 yard of .75"-wide elastic

Elastic thread

Sample in photograph knit in Crystal Palace Yarns Cotton Chenille, #9628 Purple (MC), #9598 Black (CC)

Gauge

16 sts and 26 rows = 4" <10cm> over Stockinette st

Always check gauge to save time and ensure correct yardage!

Even Coco herself would love this outfit! Chenille is one of the loveliest yarns for baby clothes—warm, soft, and washable. Do try the pantaloons as well as the sweater and hat; pants are truly easier to knit than sweaters.

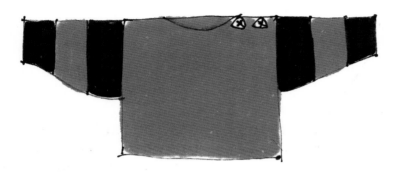

button placket, working 6 rows. Bind off firmly and evenly.

Front

Work as for back until piece measures 7.25 (8.25, 10, 11, 12)" <18.5 (21, 25.5, 28, 30.5) cm> from beg. Next RS row, work 17 (19, 21, 23, 24) sts, join 2nd ball of yarn and bind off center 5 (6, 8, 8 10) sts, work to end. Working both sides at same time, bind off from each neck edge 2 sts 3 (3, 2, 2, 2) times, dec 1 st every other row 1 (1, 3, 3, 3) times, AT THE SAME TIME, when 3 rows less than back to shoulder, work 2 buttonholes on left shoulder by yo, k2 tog, evenly spaced, beginning .5" <1.5cm> from shoulder edge. Work two more rows, and place right shoulder sts on holder for later finishing. Bind off left shoulder sts, firmly and evenly.

Sleeves

With *wrong sides facing*, place sts for both right shoulders on two parallel dpn. With a third dpn, k through first st on each needle, then the 2nd, and pass first over 2nd to bind off. Cont in this way to end for a knitted seam. On left shoulder, sew front and back together for .5" <1.5cm> from shoulder seam, catching in edge of button

SWEATER

Back

With MC, cast on 39 (44, 50, 54, 58) sts. Work in Garter st (k every row) for 1" <2.5cm>. Cont in St st, (k on RS, p on WS), until piece measures 9 (10, 12, 13, 14)" <23 (25.5, 30.5, 33, 35.5) cm> from beg, end with a WS row. On next row, work 10 (12, 14, 16, 17) sts and place on a holder for later finishing, bind off center 19 (20, 22, 22, 24) sts, p to end to form ridge. Cont in St st on left shoulder for placket. With RS facing, mark for sleeves 5 (5.5, 6, 6.25, 6.5)" <12.5 (14, 15, 16, 16.5) cm> down from shoulder seam. With RS facing and CC, pick up and k40 (44, 48, 50, 52) sts between markers. Work in St st for 5 (3, 3, 5, 5) rows. Cont in St st, dec 1 st each end of next row, then every 6th row 5 (2, 1, 8, 9) times more, every 4th row 0 (5, 7, 0, 0) times, AT SAME TIME, after 2 (2.25, 2.5, 2.75, 3)" <5 (5.5, 6.5, 7, 7.5) cm> of CC have been worked, work 2 (2.25, 2.5, 2.75, 3)" <5 (5.5, 6.5, 7, 7.5) cm> MC then cont with CC to end of sleeve. When sleeve measures 6 (6.5, 7, 8.75, 9.5)" <15 (16.5, 18, 22, 24) cm>, work 1" <2.5cm> in Garter st on 28 (28, 30, 32, 32) sts. Bind off loosely and evenly.

Finishing

Weave in all loose ends. Sew sleeve and side seams. Sew buttons to button placket.

PANT LEGS Make two

Cuff

With CC, cast on 42 (44, 48, 50, 50) sts. Work in Garter st for 1" <2.5 cm>.

Leg

Cont in St st, inc 1 st each side every 4th row 7 (8, 8, 9, 11) times, AT SAME TIME, after 2 (2.25, 2.5, 2.75, 3)" <5 (5.5, 6.5, 7, 7.5) cm> of CC, cont with MC to end of piece. Work even on 56 (60, 64, 68, 72) sts until piece measures 6 (7, 8, 9, 10)" <15 (18, 20.5, 23, 25.5) cm> from beg.

Crotch Shaping

Beg RS, bind off 3 sts beg next 0 (0, 0, 0, 2) rows, 2 sts at beg of next 2 (4, 4, 4, 2) rows. Dec 1 st each end every other row 3 (2, 3, 3, 3) times to 46 (48, 50, 54, 56) sts. With RS facing, sl sts for one leg on circular needle, place marker for center back, and sl sts of other leg to circular needle. Work even on 92 (96, 100, 108, 112) sts until piece measures 11.5 (13, 15, 16, 17.5)" <29 (33, 38, 40.5, 44.5) cm> from beg. K next rnd, dec 22 (24, 24, 26, 26) sts evenly around, to 70 (72, 76, 82, 86) sts. Work in St st for 1" <2.5cm>. P 1 rnd for turning ridge, and work in St st for 1" <2.5cm> more. Bind off.

Finishing

Sew inside leg and crotch seams. Fold band at top to WS at turning ridge and sew in place, leaving an opening for elastic. Thread elastic through opening and adjust to fit. Sew opening closed.

HAT

Circumference: Small - 17" <43cm>, Medium - 18" <45.5cm>

With MC, cast on 68 (72) sts. Work in St st for 4" <10cm>, dec 2 (0) sts on last row, to 66 (72) sts. Change to CC. Shape crown: Next row (RS): [K2 tog, k 9(10)] 6 times, to 60 (66) sts. P 1 row. Next row: [K2 tog, k8 (9)] 6 times, to 54 (60) sts. P 1 row. Cont in this way to dec 6 sts every other row, working 1 less st between decs every dec row, until there are 6 sts. Cut yarn and pull through.

Finishing

Sew back seam. Roll cuff of hat to RS and tack in place with elastic thread.

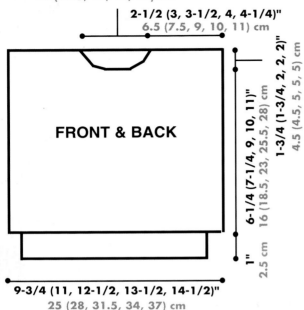

4-3/4 (5, 5-1/2, 5-1/2, 5-1/2)"
12 (12.5, 14, 14, 14) cm

2-1/2 (3, 3-1/2, 4, 4-1/4)"
6.5 (7.5, 9, 10, 11) cm

1-3/4 (1-3/4, 2, 2, 2)"
4.5 (4.5, 5, 5, 5) cm

FRONT & BACK

6-1/4 (7-1/4, 9, 10, 11)"
16 (18.5, 23, 25.5, 28) cm

1"
2.5 cm

9-3/4 (11, 12-1/2, 13-1/2, 14-1/2)"
25 (28, 31.5, 34, 37) cm

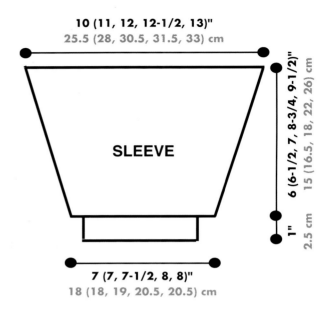

10 (11, 12, 12-1/2, 13)"
25.5 (28, 30.5, 31.5, 33) cm

SLEEVE

6 (6-1/2, 7, 8-3/4, 9-1/2)"
15 (16.5, 18, 22, 26) cm

1"
2.5 cm

7 (7, 7-1/2, 8, 8)"
18 (18, 19, 20.5, 20.5) cm

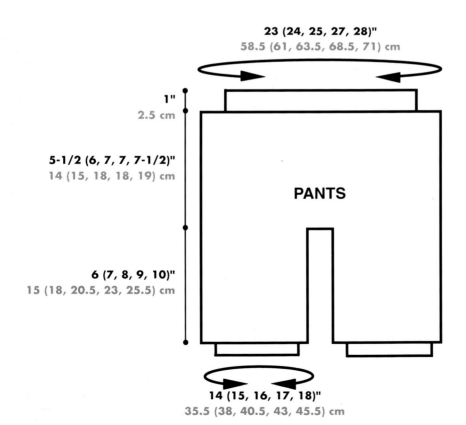

23 (24, 25, 27, 28)"
58.5 (61, 63.5, 68.5, 71) cm

1"
2.5 cm

5-1/2 (6, 7, 7, 7-1/2)"
14 (15, 18, 18, 19) cm

PANTS

6 (7, 8, 9, 10)"
15 (18, 20.5, 23, 25.5) cm

14 (15, 16, 17, 18)"
35.5 (38, 40.5, 43, 45.5) cm

Tennis Anyone?

Sizes

To fit 2 (4, 6, 8, 10) years

Finished chest, sweater:
25 (28, 30, 33, 36)"
<63.5 (71, 76, 84, 91.5) cm>

Length, shoulder to hem:
12.5 (15, 17, 18.5, 20)"
<31.5 (38, 43, 47, 51) cm>

Materials

DK weight cotton that will obtain gauge given below

350 (420, 570, 670, 770) yards <315 (378, 513, 603, 693) meters> MC

several yards or meters color A and color B

Knitting needles sizes 4 and 6 US (9 and 7 UK, 3.5 and 4.5 mm) *or size needed to obtain gauge*, circular needle size 4 US (9 UK, 3.5mm) 24 or 29" <40 or 60 cm> long

Stitch holders and markers

Cable needle (cn)

Sample in photograph knit in Rowan DK Cotton, Lettuce #241 (MC), Royal #294 (A) and Bleached White #263 (B)

Gauge

20 sts and 28 rows = 4" <10cm> over Stockinette st using larger needles

10 sts cable pat = 1.5" <4cm> using larger needles

Always check gauge to save time and ensure correct yardage!

Cable Pat (over 10 sts)

Rows 1 and 3: (RS) P2, k6, p2.

Row 2 and all WS rows: K2, p6, k2.

Row 5: P2, sl 3 sts to cn and hold to *back* of work, k3, k3 from cn, p2.

Row 7: Rep row 1.

Row 8: Rep row 2.

Rep rows 1-8 for cable pat.

Back

With smaller needles and MC, cast on 70 (78, 82, 90, 98) sts. Work in k1, p1 rib for 1.5" <4 cm>. Change to larger needles.

Establish cable pat—Next row (RS) Work 10 (12, 13, 15, 17) sts in St st (k all RS rows, p all WS rows), *work 10 sts cable pat, 10 (12, 13, 15, 17) sts in St st; rep from * twice more. Cont in pat as established until piece measures 12.5 (15, 17, 18.5, 20)" <31.5 (38, 43, 47, 51) cm> from beg. Place 21 (24, 25, 29, 33) sts on a holder for one shoulder, place next 28 (30, 32, 32, 32) sts on a 2nd holder for back neck, place rem 21 (24, 25, 29, 33) sts on a 3rd holder for other shoulder.

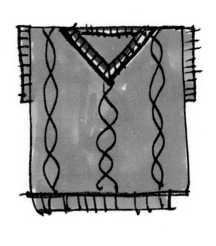

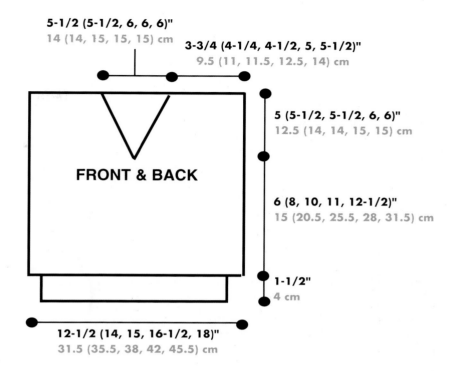

5-1/2 (5-1/2, 6, 6, 6)"
14 (14, 15, 15, 15) cm

3-3/4 (4-1/4, 4-1/2, 5, 5-1/2)"
9.5 (11, 11.5, 12.5, 14) cm

FRONT & BACK

5 (5-1/2, 5-1/2, 6, 6)"
12.5 (14, 14, 15, 15) cm

6 (8, 10, 11, 12-1/2)"
15 (20.5, 25.5, 28, 31.5) cm

1-1/2"
4 cm

12-1/2 (14, 15, 16-1/2, 18)"
31.5 (35.5, 38, 42, 45.5) cm

Front

Work as for back until piece measures 7.5 (9.5, 11.5, 12.5, 14)" <19 (24, 29, 31.5, 35.5) cm> from beg. Work V-neck as foll: Next RS row, work 33 (37, 39, 43, 47) sts, k2 tog, join 2nd ball of yarn and k2 tog, work to end. Working both sides at same time, dec 1 st at each neck edge every other row 12 (12, 14, 12, 12) times, every 4th row 1 (2, 1, 3, 3) times. Work even until same length as back. Place rem 21 (24, 25, 29, 33) sts each side on holders for later finishing.

Finishing

With *wrong sides facing*, place sts for both right shoulders on two parallel dpn. With a third dpn, k through first st on each needle, then the 2nd, and pass first over 2nd to bind off. Cont in this way to end for a knitted seam. Work left shoulder in same way. For neckband, with circular needle and A, k sts from back neck holder, pick up and k30 (33, 33, 36, 36) sts along left front neck, place marker, pick up same number of sts along right front neck, to 88 (96, 98, 104, 104) sts. Join and work in k1, p1 rib as

foll: *1 row A, 1 row B; rep from *, AT SAME TIME, dec 1 st each side of marker at center front every other row. When band measures 1" <2.5cm>, bind off all sts in rib. For armhole bands, with RS facing, mark 5.5 (6.5, 7, 7.5, 8)" <14 (16.5, 17.5, 19, 20.5) cm> down from shoulder seam. With RS facing and MC, pick up and k74 (88, 94, 102, 108) sts between markers. Work in k1, p1 rib for 1" <2.5cm>. Bind off in rib. Sew side seams, including armhole bands.

Parfait

Sizes

To fit Small/9 months - 1year
(Medium/2 - 4 years,
Large/6 years)

Finished Circumference:
16 (18, 19.5)"
<40.5 (45.5, 49.5) cm>

Materials

Mohair that will obtain gauge
given below

140 (180, 220) yards
<126 (162, 200) meters>

Knitting needles size 8 US (5
UK, 5.5mm) *or size needed to
obtain gauge.* Size G US (7 UK,
4.50mm) crochet hook.

Sample in photograph knit in Classic
Elite Mini Mohair #8558 Scarlet

Gauge

16 sts and 24 rows = 4"
<10cm> in Stockinette st.

*Always check gauge to save time
and to ensure correct yardage!*

Hat

Cast on 64 (72, 78) sts. Work in
St st (k on RS, p on WS) for 14
(16, 18)" <35.5 (40.5, 45.5)
cm>. Bind off.

Tie

With crochet hook, chain
approx 20" <51cm>. Fasten off.

Finishing

Fold piece in half widthwise and
sew back seam to form a tube.
Fold tube in half lengthwise.
Gather top of hat and weave tie
through at 1" <2.5cm> from top.
Make two large pom-poms and
sew to ends of each tie.

This little hat is knit as a tube that's folded back with a paper-bag-style top, then tied with pom-poms—very easy, very chic! Mohair is perfect for kids' wear: warm, light, fluffily soft, and strong.

Yikes! Stripes!

Sizes

To fit 6 months (1 year, 2 years, 3 years, 4 years)

Finished Chest:
24 (25.5, 27, 28, 30)"
<61 (65, 68.5, 71, 76) cm>

Length, shoulder to hem:
10.5 (11.5, 12.5, 13.5, 14.5)"
<26.5 (29, 31.5, 34.5, 37) cm>

Materials

DK weight cotton that will obtain gauge given below

For Sweater:

280 (315, 355, 450, 530) yards <252 (284, 320, 405, 478) meters> MC

45 (50, 50, 55, 55) yards <40 (45, 45, 50, 50) meters> each color A and color B

20 (25, 25, 30, 30) yards <18 (22, 22, 27, 27) meters> each color C and color D

For Pantaloons:

415 (490, 500, 525, 530) yards <374 (440, 450, 470, 475) meters> MC

20 (25, 25, 30, 30) yards <18 (22, 22, 27, 27) meters> each colors A, B, C, and D

For Cap:

105 (115, 120, 125, 130) yards <95 (105, 110, 115, 120) meters> MC

30 yards <27 meters> color A

10 yards <10 meters> each colors B, C, and D

Knitting needles size 1 US (12 UK, 2.25mm) for straps only and size 5 US (8 UK, 4mm) or size needed to obtain gauge.

Size 5 circular needle 16 (16, 24, 24, 24)" <40.5 (40.5, 61, 61, 61) cm> long for pantaloons

17 (17, 18, 19, 20)" <43 (43, 45.5, 48.5, 51) cm> of elastic 1" <2.5cm> wide for pantaloons

Stitch holders and stitch markers

Eight .5" <1.5cm> buttons

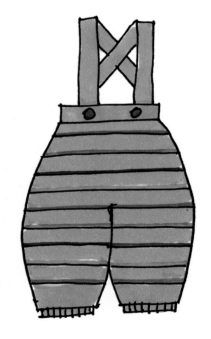

Gauge

22 sts and 28 rows = 4"
<10cm> in Stockinette st.

*Always check gauge to save time
and ensure correct yardage!*

SWEATER

Back

With size 5 needles and MC,
cast on 54 (58, 62, 66, 70) sts.
Work in k1, p1 rib for 1 (1, 1,
1.5, 1.75)" <2.5 (2.5, 2.5, 4,
4.5) cm>. P next row on WS, inc
12 sts—66 (70, 74, 78, 82) sts.
Work in St st (k on RS, p on WS)
and stripes as foll: *10 (10, 10,
12, 12) rows MC, 6 rows A; rep
from * until piece measure 10.5
(11.5, 12.5, 13.5, 14.5)" <26.5
(29, 31.5, 34.5, 37) cm> from
beg. Next row (RS): K24 (25, 27,
28, 30) sts, place on holder for
right shoulder, bind off center
18 (20, 20, 22, 22) sts for neck,
p rem 24 (25, 27, 28, 30) sts
for turning ridge. Cont to work
in St st for left back button flap
for 1" <2.5cm>. Bind off.

Front

Work same as Back, substituting
B for A until piece measures 8.5
(9.25, 10.25, 11.25, 12)" <21.5
(23.5, 26, 28.5, 30.5) cm> from
beg.

Neck Shaping (RS): Work 28 (29, 31, 32, 34) sts for left shoulder, join 2nd skein of yarn and bind off center 10 (12, 12, 14, 14) sts for neck, work to end. Working both sides at the same time, dec 1 st at each neck edge every other row 4 times—24 (25, 27, 28, 30) sts each side. Work 2 (4, 4, 4, 6) rows even. On next row, work 3 buttonholes on left shoulder (yo, k2 tog for each buttonhole) with the first one at 1" <2.5cm> from shoulder edge, the last one 2 sts from neck edge and one more buttonhole in between. Work 2 rows even. Shoulder seams: With B, *and wrong sides facing,* knit front and back tog for right shoulder seam as foll: Place sts for each shoulder on a size 5 needle. With a 3rd size 5 needle, (k first st on front needle tog with first st on back needle) twice, pass first st over 2nd st to bind off, cont in this way until all sts are bound off. For left shoulder seam, sew .5" <1.5cm> from shoulder edge.

Sleeves

Place markers on Front and Back 4 (5, 5.5, 6, 6.5)" <10 (12.5, 14, 15, 16.5) cm> down from shoulder seams for armholes. With RS facing, size 5 needles, and MC, pick up 44 (56, 60, 66, 72) sts between markers. Work stripes as for Back, but substitute C for A (for left sleeve) and D for A (for right sleeve). Work 6 rows even, then dec 1 st each end on next row, then every 4th row 4 (4, 4, 5, 4) times, then every other row 0 (5, 6, 6, 9) times—34 (36, 38, 42, 44) sts. Work even until sleeve measures 4.75 (5.5, 5.75, 6.25, 6.5)" <12 (14, 14.5, 16, 16.5) cm> from pick-up row, dec 4 sts evenly across last row. With MC, work in k1, p1 rib for 4 rows. Bind off loosely in rib.

Finishing

Neckband: With RS facing, size 5 needles, and MC, pick up and k72 (76, 76, 82, 84) sts evenly around neck edge. Work in k1, p1 rib for 3 (3, 5, 5, 5) rows. Next row (RS): Rib 2, yo, k2 tog (buttonhole), rib to end. Rib 2 rows more. Bind off in rib. Sew side and sleeve seams. Sew on buttons.

PANTALOONS

Legs (make 2)

With size 5 needles and MC, cast on 60 (64, 68, 72, 76) sts. Work in k1, p1 rib for 2.5 (2.5, 2.5, 3, 3)" <6.5 (6.5, 6.5, 7.5, 7.5) cm>, inc 20 (24, 28, 28, 28) sts evenly across last row—80 (88, 96, 100, 104) sts. Work in St st (k on RS, p on WS) and stripes as foll: *10 rows MC, 2 rows B, 10 rows MC, 2 rows D, 10 rows MC, 2 rows C, 10 rows MC, 2 rows A, rep from * until piece measures 9.5 (10, 10.5, 12, 13.25)" <24 (25.5, 26.5, 30.5, 33.5) cm> from beg. Crotch: Bind off 4 (4, 5, 6 6) sts at beg of next 2 rows, 1 st at beg of next 6 rows—66 (74, 80, 82, 86) sts.

Body

With RS of both legs facing, place sts of both legs on size 5 circular needle, join and place marker for beg of rnd—132 (148, 160, 164, 172) sts. Cont in St st (k every rnd) and stripe pat until piece measures 14.5 (15.5, 17, 19, 20)" <37 (39.5, 43, 48.5, 51) cm> from beg. Waistband: With MC, *k 2, k2 tog; rep from * to end. Work in St st for 7 rnds. P one rnd for turning ridge. Work in St st for 7 rnds. Place sts on a length of yarn.

Straps (for sizes 6 months, 1 year, and 2 years)

With size 1 needle and MC, cast on 8 sts and work in k1, p1 rib for 3 rows. Next row: Rib 3, yo, k2 tog (buttonhole), rib to end. Cont rib for 12 (14, 16)" <30.5 (35, 40.5) cm>. Make a buttonhole as before. Rib 3 rows. Bind off in rib.

Finishing

Sew crotch, then leg seams. Fold waistband at turning ridge to WS and sew sts to inside waistband, leaving an opening for elastic. Weave elastic through casing, adjust to fit and sew casing closed. Sew on buttons if necessary.

CAP

With size 5 needles and MC, cast on 65 (68, 70, 75, 80) sts and work in k1, p1 rib for 2.5" <6.5cm>. Work in stripes as on Pantaloons, but work 5 rows MC instead of 10 until 30 (30, 32, 34, 34) rows have been worked above rib—piece measures approx 6.75 (7, 7, 7.5, 7.5)" <17 (18, 18, 19, 19) cm> from beg. Next row: *K2, k2 tog, rep from *, end k1 (0, 2, 3, 0)—49 (51, 53, 57, 60) sts. Work one row even. Next row: *K2, k2 tog, rep from *, end k1 (3, 1, 1, 0)—37 (39, 40, 43, 45) sts. Work one row even. Next row:

*K2 tog, rep from *, end k1 (1, 0, 1, 1)—19 (20, 20, 22, 23) sts. Work 1 row even. Next row: *K2 tog, rep from *, end k1 (0, 0, 0, 1). Cut yarn, pull through rem sts and sew back seam. Tassel: Wind 25 yds <23m> B around a 3" <7.5cm> cardboard rectangle. With 10" <25.5cm> yarn, pull through and tie firmly. With 8" <20.5cm> yarn, wind around tassel 1" <2.5cm> from tie end. Cut other end, trim evenly. Sew to top of Cap.

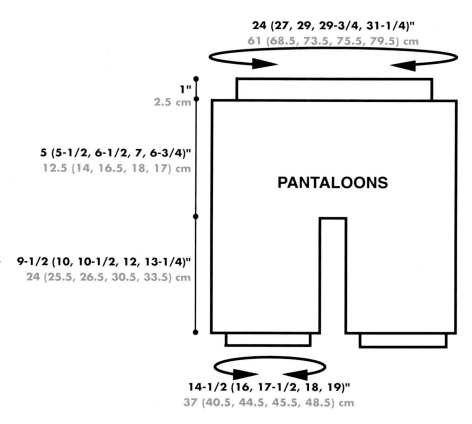

24 (27, 29, 29-3/4, 31-1/4)"
61 (68.5, 73.5, 75.5, 79.5) cm

1"
2.5 cm

5 (5-1/2, 6-1/2, 7, 6-3/4)"
12.5 (14, 16.5, 18, 17) cm

PANTALOONS

9-1/2 (10, 10-1/2, 12, 13-1/4)"
24 (25.5, 26.5, 30.5, 33.5) cm

14-1/2 (16, 17-1/2, 18, 19)"
37 (40.5, 44.5, 45.5, 48.5) cm

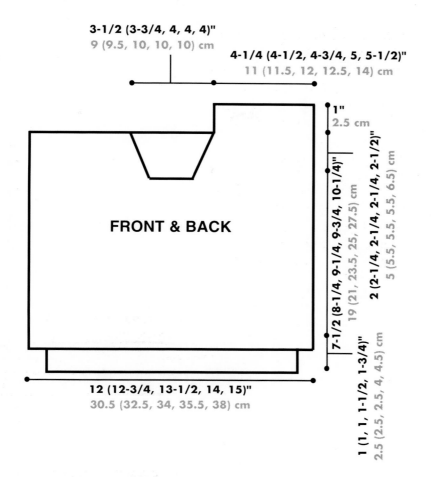

3-1/2 (3-3/4, 4, 4, 4)"
9 (9.5, 10, 10, 10) cm

4-1/4 (4-1/2, 4-3/4, 5, 5-1/2)"
11 (11.5, 12, 12.5, 14) cm

1"
2.5 cm

2 (2-1/4, 2-1/4, 2-1/4, 2-1/2)"
5 (5.5, 5.5, 5.5, 6.5) cm

FRONT & BACK

7-1/2 (8-1/4, 9-1/4, 9-3/4, 10-1/4)"
19 (21, 23.5, 25, 27.5) cm

1 (1, 1, 1-1/2, 1-3/4)"
2.5 (2.5, 2.5, 4, 4.5) cm

12 (12-3/4, 13-1/2, 14, 15)"
30.5 (32.5, 34, 35.5, 38) cm

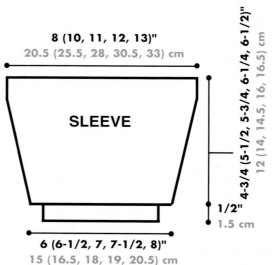

8 (10, 11, 12, 13)"
20.5 (25.5, 28, 30.5, 33) cm

SLEEVE

4-3/4 (5-1/2, 5-3/4, 6-1/4, 6-1/2)"
12 (14, 14.5, 16, 16.5) cm

1/2"
1.5 cm

6 (6-1/2, 7, 7-1/2, 8)"
15 (16.5, 18, 19, 20.5) cm

HOLIDAYS

Christmas, Hanukkah, Easter, the Fourth of July, or a special birthday party—whatever the occasion, a hand-knitted outfit stands out in the crowd. Beautifully crafted dressy dresses, sweaters, and pants can be passed on from child to child, so choose the very best fibers for these holiday outfits—and add a little heirloom to your holidays.

La Pinafore

Sizes

1 year (2 years, 4 years)

Finished chest:
19.25 (22, 25)"
<49 (56, 63.5) cm>

Length, shoulder to hem:
18 (22, 25)"
<45 (56, 64) cm>

Materials

DK weight cotton that will
obtain gauge given below

610 (820, 1070) yards
<550 (738, 964) meters>

Knitting needles (straight and
dp) size 5 US (UK 8, 4mm), *or
size needed to obtain gauge*

Crochet hook, size F US (8 UK,
4mm)

Three 5/8" <1.5cm> buttons

Gauge

22 sts and 28 rows = 4"
<10cm> over Stockinette st

*Always check gauge to save time
and ensure correct yardage!*

Reminiscent of the classic styles of grandmother's day, this simple pinafore has ruffled shoulders and an open back. Charming over a light cotton day dress, it could also be seamed up the back as a sundress, for those warm summer garden parties.

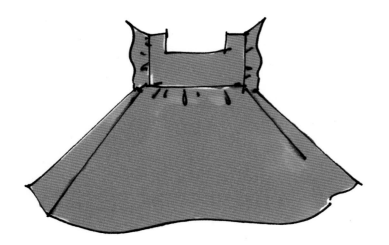

Pattern Stitch

Rows 1 and 3 (WS): Purl.

Row 2: *P1, k5; rep from *.

Row 4: *K3, p1, k2; rep from *.

Rep rows 1-4 for pat st.

Skirt

Hem: Cast on 212 (244, 276) sts. Work in St st, (k on RS, p on WS) for 7 rows. Picot turning ridge: On RS, k 1 st, *k2 tog, yarn over (yo); rep from *, ending with k1. Next row: P across. Cont in St st until piece measures 12.5 (15, 17)" <32 (38, 43) cm> from turning ridge, ending on WS row.

Yoke

K2 tog across to 106 (122, 138) sts. Divide for front and backs and work in pat st as foll: work 28 (32, 36) sts for left back, join another skein of yarn and work 50 (58, 66) sts for front, join another skein of yarn and work 28 (32, 36) sts for right back. Work each section at once with separate skeins of yarn. *At the same time,* work buttonhole on right side on the 4th row by k3, k2 tog, yo, work to end. Work 2 more buttonholes at 1 (1.25, 1.5)" <2.5 (3, 4) cm> intervals. When yoke measures 3 (3.5, 4)" <7.5 (9, 10) cm>, end with a WS row and work as foll: bind off first 15 (18, 20) sts of left back, work 11 (12, 14) sts for strap, bind off rem 2 sts of left back; bind off first 3 sts of front, work 11 (12, 14) sts for strap, bind off 22 (28, 32) sts, work 11 (12, 14) sts for strap, bind off rem 3 sts of front, bind off first 2 sts of right back, work 11 (12, 14) sts for strap, bind off rem 15 (18, 20) sts.

Straps

Working each strap separately, cont even in pat st until strap measures 2.5 (3.5, 4)" <6.5 (9, 10) cm>. Knit shoulder seams tog as foll: with WS facing, place front and back right shoulder sts on parallel size 5 dp needles. With a third size 5 needle, knit the first st of both needles tog, then *knit the next st of both needles tog, and pass second st over first; rep from * to end. Rep for left strap.

Ruffle

Place markers 5 (5.5, 6.75)" <12.5 (14, 17) cm> down from shoulders on front and back for armholes. With RS facing and dp needles, pick up and k70 (78, 96) sts evenly around armhole between markers. P next row, inc 1 st in each st—140 (156, 192) sts. Without joining, work back and forth in k4, p4 rib until ruffle measures 2.5 (3, 3.25)" <6.5 (7.5, 8.5) cm>. Bind off in rib.

Finishing

Fold hem up on turning ridge and tack in place. Pull ruffle down, and tack in place under armhole opening. With crochet hook, work picot edge evenly around neckline and back edges as foll: *sc in 2 sts, ch 3, sl st in 3rd ch from hook, rep from *. Sew buttons in place.

2 (2, 2-1/2)"
5 (5, 6.5) cm

3 (3-1/2, 4)" 7.5 (9, 10) cm

2-1/2 (3-1/2, 4)" 6.5 (9, 10) cm

9-1/2 (11, 12-1/2)"
24 (28, 31.5) cm

**FRONT & BACK
SKIRT**

12-1/2 (15, 17)"
32 (38, 43) cm

38-1/2 (44, 50)"
98 (112, 127) cm

Party Dress

Sizes

To fit 3-6 months (1 year, 2 years, 3 years)

Finished chest:
16 (18, 20, 22)"
<40.5 (45.5, 51, 56) cm>

Length, shoulder to hem:
13 (15, 16.5, 18.5)"
<33 (38, 42, 47) cm>

Materials

Worsted weight cotton chenille (color A), cotton/rayon blend (color B), and fingering weight cotton for collar (color C) that will obtain gauge given below

110 (130, 160, 180) yards <100 (117, 145, 162) meters> color A

270 (390, 480, 540) yards <245 (350, 435, 486 meters> color B

41 (61, 78, 110) yards <37 (54, 70, 100) meters> color C

Knitting needles one pair size 6 US (7 UK, 4.5mm) *or size needed to obtain gauge.*

Size 6 circular needle, 24" <61cm> long

Knitting needles size 3 US (UK 10, 3.25mm) for collar

3 (4, 5, 5) pearl bead buttons

Stitch holders and stitch markers

Sample in photograph knit in Crystal Palace Chenille, Caprice, and Baby Georgia, Black (A), Teal (B) and White (C)

This dress combines soft chenille for the bodice and trim with a dressier cotton blend for the skirt and sleeves. The crisp, white, French collar tops off this tea-dress look for your little party girl.

Gauge

16 sts and 20 rows = 4"
<10cm> over Stockinette st in
chenille

20 sts and 26 rows = 4"
<10cm> over Stockinette st in
cotton blend

*Always check gauge to save time
and ensure correct yardage!*

Pattern Stitches

Stockinette St

K 1 row on RS, p 1 row on WS.
K each row when working in the
round.

Reverse Stockinette St

P 1 row on RS, k 1 row on WS.

Seed Stitch

*K1, p1; rep from * across row.
Next row, p all k sts, k all p sts.
Rep last row for Seed st.

Skirt

With circular needle and A, cast
on 128 (144, 160, 176) sts,
and place marker for end of
rnd. (K1 rnd, p1 rnd) 3 times
for Garter st. Join B and work 6
rnds in Seed st. Rep these 12
rnds once more, and work 6
more rnds Garter st with A.
Cont in St st with B only until
piece measures 9 (10, 10.5,
11.5)" <23 (25, 26.5, 29) cm>
from beg. On next rnd, k2 tog
around to 64 (72, 80, 88) sts.

Front Bodice

Divide sts in half for front and
back bodice. Place half the sts
on a holder. With single pointed
needles and A, work separately
on rem 32 (36, 40, 44) sts for
front bodice in rev St st for 2
(2.5, 3, 4)" <5 (6.5, 7.5, 10)
cm>.

Neck shaping

Work 11 (13, 14, 16) sts, attach
2nd ball and bind off center 10
(10, 12, 12) sts, work to end.
Dec 1 st each side at neck edge
every other row 4 times. Work
even until bodice measures 4 (5,
6, 7)" <10 (13, 15, 18) cm>.
Place rem 7 (9, 10, 12) sts each
side on holders for later finishing.

Back Bodice

Work first 16 (18, 20, 22) sts from back holder, join 2nd ball of yarn and work rem sts from holder. Work as for front, omitting neck shaping, until same length as front bodice. Knit shoulder seams tog as foll: Place sts for each right shoulder on two needles. With WS of pieces tog and a 3rd needle, k through the first st on each needle, then the 2nd and pass the first over the 2nd to bind off. Cont in this way until all shoulder sts have been bound off. Work in same way for the left shoulder.

Sleeves

With straight needles and B, cast on 32 (34, 36, 38) sts, and work 4 rows Seed st for cuff. Next RS row, inc 1 st in each st to 64 (68, 72, 76) sts. Cont in St st, inc 4 (5, 5, 5) sts evenly across row every other row 6 (11, 15, 10) times, then inc 5 (6, 0, 6) sts evenly across row every other row 4 (2, 0, 6) times, to 108 (135, 147, 162) sts. Work even, if necessary, until piece measures 3 (4, 4.5, 5)" <7.5 (10, 11.5, 12.5) cm> above cuff, end with a WS row. K3 tog and bind off at the same time. Weave in all loose ends. With RS tog, sew sleeve seam. Pin sleeve into armhole opening, and sew.

Collar

With RS facing, C, and size 3 needles, beg at back left shoulder, pick up and k56 (56, 60, 60) sts evenly around neck edge. Work 4 rows Garter st. Work 28 (28, 30, 30) sts, join 2nd ball of yarn and work to end. Working both sides at once, cont in St st, and inc 4 sts unevenly across row on each side of collar, every other row 3 (3, 4, 4) times to 40 (40, 46, 46) sts each side. Work even until collar measures 2 (2, 2.5, 2.5)" <5 (5, 6.5, 6.5) cm> above Garter st. Work eyelets as foll: K1, *yo, sl 1, k1, psso; rep from * end, k1. Next row, p. Bind off

evenly and firmly. Crochet a picot edge around collar as foll: *sc in 2 sts, ch 3, sl st in first ch, sk 1 st; rep from *.

Finishing

Weave in all loose ends. Sew pearl buttons evenly along left back edge. With crochet hook, work 1 row sc along back openings, making a button loop opposite buttons.

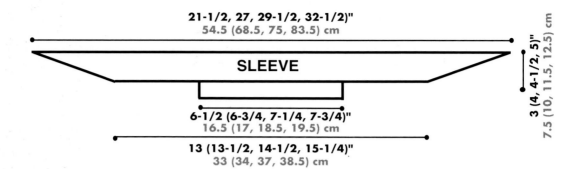

21-1/2, 27, 29-1/2, 32-1/2)"
54.5 (68.5, 75, 83.5) cm

SLEEVE

3 (4, 4-1/2, 5)"
7.5 (10, 11.5, 12.5) cm

6-1/2 (6-3/4, 7-1/4, 7-3/4)"
16.5 (17, 18.5, 19.5) cm

13 (13-1/2, 14-1/2, 15-1/4)"
33 (34, 37, 38.5) cm

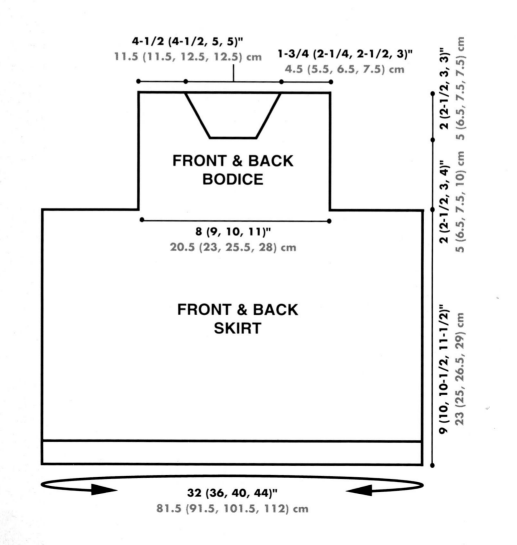

4-1/2 (4-1/2, 5, 5)"
11.5 (11.5, 12.5, 12.5) cm

1-3/4 (2-1/4, 2-1/2, 3)"
4.5 (5.5, 6.5, 7.5) cm

2 (2-1/2, 3, 3)"
5 (6.5, 7.5, 7.5) cm

FRONT & BACK
BODICE

2 (2-1/2, 3, 4)"
5 (6.5, 7.5, 10) cm

8 (9, 10, 11)"
20.5 (23, 25.5, 28) cm

FRONT & BACK
SKIRT

9 (10, 10-1/2, 11-1/2)"
23 (25, 26.5, 29) cm

32 (36, 40, 44)"
81.5 (91.5, 101.5, 112) cm

Petite Chic

Sizes

To fit 6 months (1 year,
2 years, 4 years, 6 years)

Finished chest:
16 (18, 21, 24, 28)"
<41 (46, 53, 61, 71) cm>

Length, shoulder to hem:
15.5 (19, 23, 26, 29)"
<39 (48, 58, 66, 73.5) cm>

Materials

DK weight cotton that will
obtain gauge given below

350 (490, 700, 900, 1200)
yards <315 (440, 630, 810,
1,080) meters> MC

100 (100, 100, 150,150) yards
<90 (90, 90, 135, 135) meters>
CC

Knitting needles, one pair
straight size 5 US (UK 8, 4mm),
one pair double pointed size 5

Size 5 circular needle, 20 or 26"
<51 or 66cm> long

Two 1" <2.5cm> round buttons

Bobbins

*Spring and
summer parties
offer the perfect
opportunity for
this adorable,
short-sleeved
dress in cool
cotton. It may
be knit with
bobbins in the
intarsia method
or by carrying
colors across.
The bold polka
dots pay
homage to
Merimekko,
one of my
early design
inspirations.*

Gauge

22 sts and 28 rows = 4"
<10cm> in Stockinette st.

*Always check gauge to save time
and ensure correct yardage!*

Skirt

With circular needles and MC,
cast on 176 (200, 232, 264,
308) sts. Work back and forth
as with straight needles as foll:
Work 7 (7, 7, 9, 9) rows in St st
(k on RS, p on WS). K next row
on WS for folding ridge for hem.
Work 8 rows more in St st, then
continue in polka dot pat as
foll: (Note: chart is drawn for 1-
year size, that is, there are 25
MC sts between dots. Use a separate bobbin of yarn for each
block of color.) Work 25 sts dot
(first 25 sts of chart), 19 (25,
33, 27, 37) sts MC, 25 sts dot,
19 (25, 33, 28, 36) sts MC, 25
sts dot, 19 (25, 33, 28, 37) sts
MC, 25 sts dot, 19 (25, 33, 28,
36) sts MC, 0 (0, 0, 25, 25) sts
dot, 0 (0, 0, 28, 37) sts MC.
Cont in pat as established until
all chart rows have been
worked, then cont with MC only
until piece measures 10 (13,
16, 17, 18)" <25 (33, 41, 43,
46) cm> from folding ridge, end
with a WS row. Next row: K2 tog
across to 88 (100, 116, 132,
154) sts. Next row: P44 (50, 58,
66, 77) and place on a holder
for back, p to end for front.
Cont on straight needles.

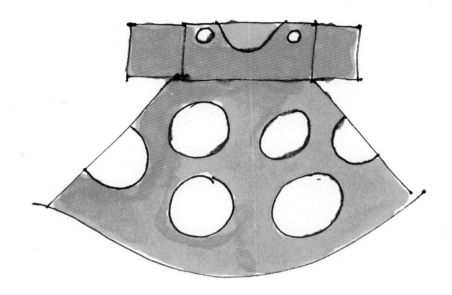

Front Bodice

Work front sts in St st for 2.5
(3, 4, 6, 8)" <6.5 (7.5, 10, 15,
20) cm>, ending with a WS row.
Neck shaping: Work 16 (18, 21,
24, 28) sts, join a second skein
of yarn and bind off center 12
(14, 16, 18, 21) sts, work to
end. Working both sides at the
same time, dec 1 st at each
neck edge every other row 5
times. 11 (13, 16, 19, 23) sts
each side. On next row, RS,
work buttonholes at 2 sts in
from neck edge by binding off 3
sts. Next row, cast on 3 sts over
buttonhole. Work 2 rows even,
and bind off evenly on RS.

Back Bodice

Work as for front, omitting neck
shaping and buttonholes. On
last RS row, k11 (13, 16, 19,
23) sts, join 2nd skein of yarn
and p next 22 (24, 26, 28, 31)
sts and place on holder for
back neck, k to end. Working
both sides at same time, cont in
St st for 6 (6, 6, 8, 8) rows for
button placket, and bind off.

Sleeves

With RS facing, dpn, and MC,
pick up and k50 (55, 66, 88,
110) sts around arm opening. K
and work even to 3.5 (4, 5, 6,
8)" <9 (10, 13, 15, 20) cm>. P 1
rnd, k 5 rnds. Place sts on yarn
for later finishing.

Finishing

Neckline

With circular needle, working back and forth, pick up and k45 (50, 60, 66, 77) sts across front shoulders and neckline. K 3 rows, and bind off firmly and evenly. Rep across back neckline. Sew shoulders 1 (1, 2, 3, 4)" <2.5 (2.5, 5, 7.5, 10) cm> from shoulder edge. Sew button to back button flap. Sew one side seam on skirt.

Hem

Fold hem on turning ridge, and hem with easy tension. Sew hems on sleeves in the same way.

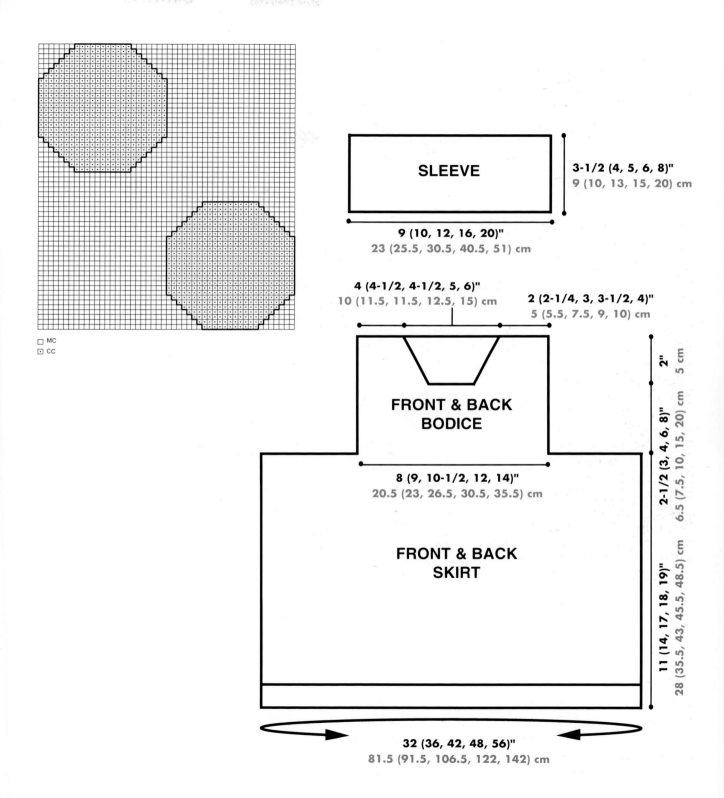

□ MC
⊡ CC

SLEEVE

3-1/2 (4, 5, 6, 8)"
9 (10, 13, 15, 20) cm

9 (10, 12, 16, 20)"
23 (25.5, 30.5, 40.5, 51) cm

4 (4-1/2, 4-1/2, 5, 6)"
10 (11.5, 11.5, 12.5, 15) cm

2 (2-1/4, 3, 3-1/2, 4)"
5 (5.5, 7.5, 9, 10) cm

**FRONT & BACK
BODICE**

8 (9, 10-1/2, 12, 14)"
20.5 (23, 26.5, 30.5, 35.5) cm

**FRONT & BACK
SKIRT**

2"
5 cm

2-1/2 (3, 4, 6, 8)"
6.5 (7.5, 10, 15, 20) cm

11 (14, 17, 18, 19)"
28 (35.5, 43, 45.5, 48.5) cm

32 (36, 42, 48, 56)"
81.5 (91.5, 106.5, 122, 142) cm

Holiday Dress

Sizes

To fit 6 months (1 year, 2 years, 4 years, 6 years)

Finished Chest:
15 (16, 18, 21.5, 24)"
<38 (40.5, 45.5, 54, 61) cm>

Length from shoulder to hem:
13.5 (15, 16.5, 19.75, 25.5)"
<34.5 (38, 42, 50, 65) cm>
including zigzag hem

Materials

DK weight cotton that will obtain gauge given below

550 (645, 800, 1220, 1690) yards <495 (580, 720, 1,098, 1,675) meters> MC

50 yards <45 meters> CC

Knitting needles one pair and one set double pointed size 5 US (8 UK, 4mm) *or size needed to obtain gauge.*

Size 5 circular needle 20" <51cm> long

Six pearl half-round buttons

Stitch holders and stitch markers

Gauge

22 sts and 28 rows = 4" <10cm> in Stockinette st.

Always check gauge to save time and ensure correct yardage!

Dress patterns are hard to find, and this one is much easier to knit than it looks! The fanciful hem is made with individual triangles strung together on a circular needle. Worked up in pure white, the dress would make a sweet christening gown.

Zigzag Hem

With size 5 straight needles cast on 2 sts. Work in Garter st, inc 1 st at end of every row until there are 14 (15, 16, 18, 18) sts. Make a total of 14 (14, 15, 16, 18) triangles. Place sts on circular needle. Join and place marker for beg of rnd—196 (210, 240, 288, 324) sts. K 1 rnd, p 1 rnd, k 1 rnd. *K 3 (3, 3, 4, 5) rnds, p 3 (3, 3, 4, 5) rnds; rep from * twice more. Cont in St st (k every rnd) for 6 (7, 8, 10.25, 12.5)" <15 (18, 20.5, 26, 31.5) cm>.

Bodice

Next Rnd: K2 tog around—98 (105, 120, 144, 162) sts. Work in k1, p1 rib for 2 rnds, dec 1 st for size 1 year only. Divide for front and back: With straight size 5 needles, work 49 (52, 60, 72, 81) sts for front, place rem sts on a holder for back. Working back and forth on front sts only, cont rib for 2.25 (2.5, 3, 3.75, 5.5)" <5.5 (6.5, 7.5, 9.5, 14) cm>. Neck shaping: Work 21 (22, 25, 30, 34) sts, join 2nd skein of yarn and bind off center 7 (8, 10, 12, 13) sts for neck, work to end. Working both sides at same time, dec 1 st at each neck edge every other row 8 (8, 8, 9, 10) times, AT THE SAME TIME, when bodice measures 4 (4.5, 5, 6, 8)" <10 (11.5, 12.5, 15, 20.5)

cm>, work buttonholes on left side of front as foll: Next (buttonhole) row: Rib 2 (2, 3, 3, 3), yo, k2 tog, (rib 2 (2, 3, 5, 6), yo, k2 tog) twice, rib to end. Work even until bodice measures 4.5 (5, 5.5, 6.5, 8.5)" <11.5 (12.5, 14, 16.5, 21.5) cm>. Bind off left shoulder sts and place right shoulder sts on a holder.

Back

Work as for front, omitting neck shaping and buttonholes, and working last row as foll: Next row (RS): Work 13 (14, 17, 21, 24) sts and place on a holder for right shoulder, bind off next 23 (24, 26, 30, 33) sts for neck, work to end. Cont on rem 13 (14, 17, 21, 24) sts in St st for left back button flap for 1" <2.5cm>. Bind off. Right shoulder seams: Knit front and back tog for right shoulder seam as foll: Place sts of each right shoulder on a size 5 needle to work sts from the RS. With a 3rd size 5 needle, (k first st on front needle tog with first st on back needle) twice, pass first st over 2nd st to bind off, cont in this way until all sts are bound off.

Sleeves

Place markers on front and back 4 (4.25, 4.5, 5, 6)" <10 (11, 11.5, 12.5, 15) cm> down from shoulder seams for armholes. With RS facing, size 5 double pointed needles and MC, pick up and k44 (46, 48, 56, 68) sts between markers. Join and place marker at underarm. Work in St st (k every rnd) for 2.5 (3, 4, 5, 5.75)" <6.5 (7.5, 10, 12.5, 14.5) cm>. Dec 1 st each end of next rnd (by knitting 2 tog *before* and *after* marker), then every other rnd 7 (7, 8, 9, 13) times more—28 (30, 30, 36, 40) sts. P 3 (3, 3, 5, 5) rnds, k 3 (3, 3, 5, 5) rnds, p 3 (3, 3, 5, 5) rnds. Bind off purlwise.

Finishing

Collar: With RS facing, size 5 straight needles, and CC, beg at top of left front shoulder, pick up 56 (60, 64, 72, 78) sts evenly around neck edge. Work in k1, p1 rib for 2 rows, inc 5 sts evenly across last row. Cont in Garter st as foll: Next Row (WS): K43 (47, 48, 54, 59), join 2nd skein of yarn and k18 (18, 21, 23, 24). Work both sides at same time for 16 (16, 18, 18, 20) rows more. Bind off. Make 3 button loops on left front collar edge. Sew buttons to shoulder and collar.

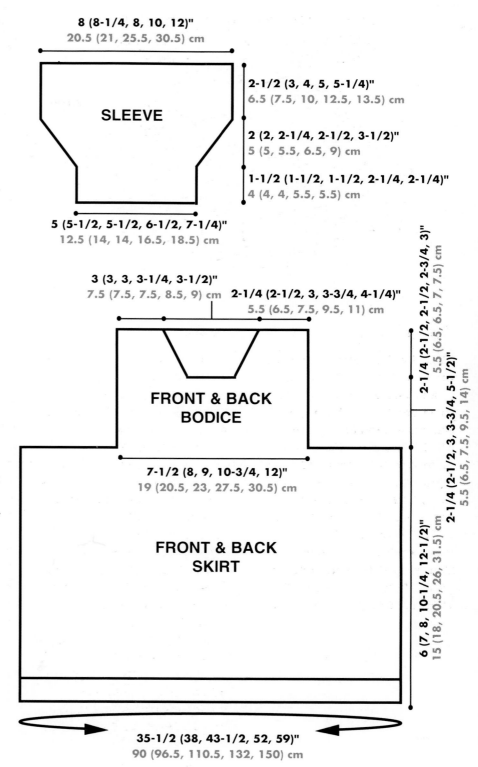

8 (8-1/4, 8, 10, 12)"
20.5 (21, 25.5, 30.5) cm

SLEEVE

2-1/2 (3, 4, 5, 5-1/4)"
6.5 (7.5, 10, 12.5, 13.5) cm

2 (2, 2-1/4, 2-1/2, 3-1/2)"
5 (5, 5.5, 6.5, 9) cm

1-1/2 (1-1/2, 1-1/2, 2-1/4, 2-1/4)"
4 (4, 4, 5.5, 5.5) cm

5 (5-1/2, 5-1/2, 6-1/2, 7-1/4)"
12.5 (14, 14, 16.5, 18.5) cm

3 (3, 3, 3-1/4, 3-1/2)"
7.5 (7.5, 7.5, 8.5, 9) cm

2-1/4 (2-1/2, 3, 3-3/4, 4-1/4)"
5.5 (6.5, 7.5, 9.5, 11) cm

FRONT & BACK BODICE

2-1/4 (2-1/2, 2-1/2, 2-3/4, 3)"
5.5 (6.5, 6.5, 7, 7.5) cm

2-1/4 (2-1/2, 3, 3-3/4, 5-1/2)"
5.5 (6.5, 7.5, 9.5, 14) cm

7-1/2 (8, 9, 10-3/4, 12)"
19 (20.5, 23, 27.5, 30.5) cm

FRONT & BACK SKIRT

6 (7, 8, 10-1/4, 12-1/2)"
15 (18, 20.5, 26, 31.5) cm

35-1/2 (38, 43-1/2, 52, 59)"
90 (96.5, 110.5, 132, 150) cm

Classic Brit Jacket

Sizes

To fit 2 years (4 years, 6 years, 8 years)

Finished chest, buttoned:
25.5 (28, 30.5, 33)"
<65 (71, 77.5, 84) cm>

Length, shoulder to hem:
13 (14, 15, 16)"
<33 (35.5, 38, 40.5) cm>

Materials

Bulky weight wool that will obtain gauge given below

305 (375, 425, 485) yards
<274 (338, 382, 436) meters>

Knitting needles size 7 US (6 UK, 4.5mm) and 9 US (4 UK, 6mm) *or size needed to obtain gauge*

Crochet hook size J US (4 UK, 6mm)

Stitch holders

Four .5" <1.5cm> buttons

Sample in photograph knit in Manos del Urugauy

Gauge

14 sts and 20 rows = 4"
<10cm> over Stockinette st

Always check gauge to save time and ensure correct yardage!

Simple patterns can be deceiving! Wonderful yarn and the right buttons make this bulky weight double-breasted jacket a special sweater. My son, Alexander, wore this jacket for many holidays over a white shirt with shorts and knee socks, looking just like an English schoolboy. The pattern also makes up well in mohair.

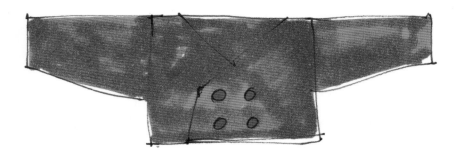

Back

With smaller needles, cast on 38 (44, 49, 54) sts and work in k1, p1 rib for 6 (6, 8, 8) rows. Change to larger needles, and inc 6 sts evenly across row, to 44 (50, 55, 60) sts. Work in St st, (k on RS, p on WS) until piece measures 13 (14, 15, 16)" <33 (35.5, 38, 40.5) cm> from the beg. Place 15 (17, 19, 21) sts on holder, bind off center 14 (16, 17, 18) sts for neck, place rem 15 (17, 19, 21) sts on holder for later finishing.

Right Front

With smaller needles, cast on 27 (29, 31, 33) sts, and work rib as for back. Change to larger needles and work in St st, inc 4 sts evenly across row, to 31 (33, 35, 37) sts. Cont until piece measures 5 (5.5, 6, 6.5)" <12.5 (14, 15, 16.5) cm> from beg. Beg dec for V-neck as foll: dec 1 st at neck edge (k1, k2 tog), at beg of every RS row 15 (13, 12, 11) times, then every

4th row 1 (3, 4, 5) times. Cont even on 15 (17, 19, 21) sts until same length as back. Place shoulder sts on holder for later finishing.

Left Front

Work as for Right Front, reversing shaping. At the same time, place buttonholes as foll: Work 6 (6, 8, 8) rows ribbing. Work inc row. In next row, on WS, p1, p2 tog, yo, p7 (9, 11, 13), p2 tog, yo, p to end. Place next set of buttonholes in row just below neck shaping. *With WS facing*, place right shoulder sts from holder on two size 9 needles. With a third size 9 needle, k the first st on front needle tog with first st on back needle, *k next st on front and back needles tog, sl the first st over 2nd st to bind off; rep from * until all sts are bound off. Work left shoulder sts in same way.

Sleeves

With RS facing, place markers 6.5 (7, 7.5, 8)" <16.5 (18, 19, 20.5) cm> down from shoulder seam on front and back. Pick up and k46 (49, 53, 56) sts evenly between markers. Work in St st as follows: work 6 rows even. Dec 1 st each side of next row, then every 4th row 9 (11, 11, 11) times more, then every other row 1 (0, 1, 2) times to 24 (25, 27, 28) sts. Change to smaller needles, and dec 4 sts evenly in first row on RS. Work k1, p1 rib for 6 (6, 8, 8) rows. Bind off in rib, loosely.

Finishing

Sew sleeve and side seams. Weave all loose ends into back of work. Single crochet around V-neck and front edges. Sew buttons in place.

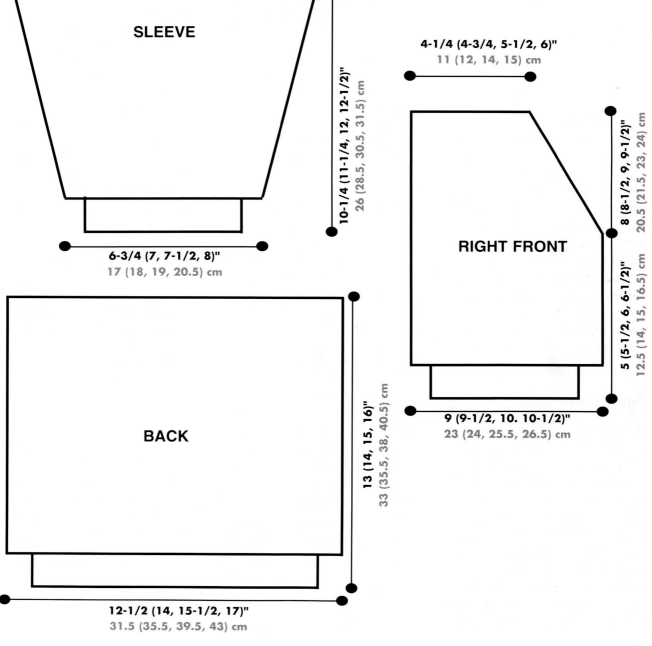

SLEEVE

13 (14, 15, 16)"
33 (35.5, 38, 40.5) cm

1"
2.5 cm

10-1/4 (11-1/4, 12, 12-1/2)"
26 (28.5, 30.5, 31.5) cm

6-3/4 (7, 7-1/2, 8)"
17 (18, 19, 20.5) cm

BACK

13 (14, 15, 16)"
33 (35.5, 38, 40.5) cm

12-1/2 (14, 15-1/2, 17)"
31.5 (35.5, 39.5, 43) cm

RIGHT FRONT

4-1/4 (4-3/4, 5-1/2, 6)"
11 (12, 14, 15) cm

8 (8-1/2, 9, 9-1/2)"
20.5 (21.5, 23, 24) cm

5 (5-1/2, 6, 6-1/2)"
12.5 (14, 15, 16.5) cm

9 (9-1/2, 10. 10-1/2)"
23 (24, 25.5, 26.5) cm

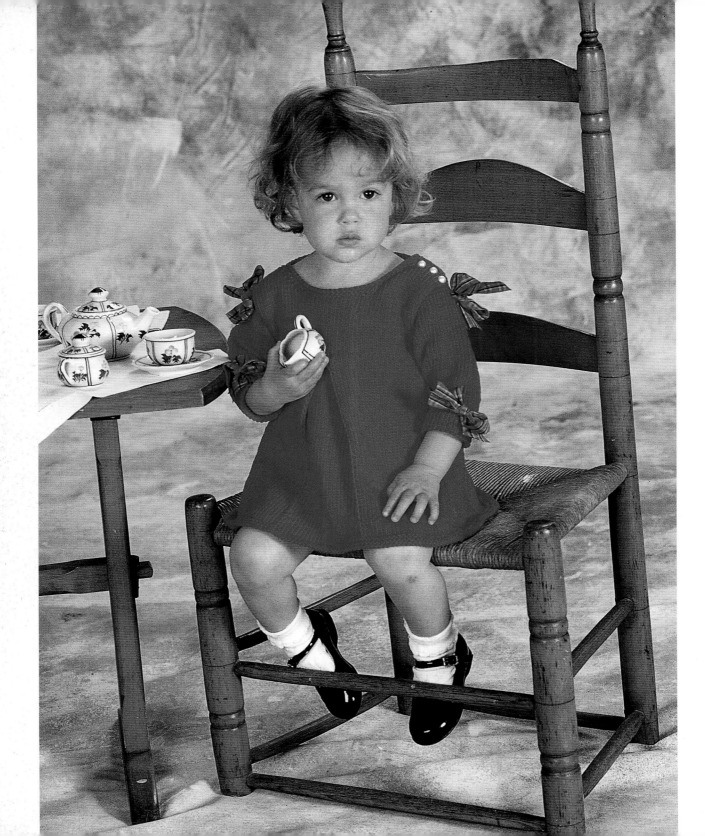

Buttons and Bows

Sizes

To fit 3 months (6 months, 1 year, 2 years, 4 years, 6 years)

Finished chest:
14.5 (15.25, 16.75, 18, 21, 24)"
<37 (38, 42.5, 45.5, 53.5, 61) cm>

Length, shoulder to hem:
12 (12.5, 14, 15.5, 18.5, 22.5)"
<30.5 (32, 35.5, 39.5, 47, 57) cm>

Materials

DK weight cotton that will obtain gauge given below

310 (320, 340, 360, 400, 440) yards <280 (288, 306, 324, 360, 396) meters>

Knitting needles, one pair straight and one set (4) double pointed needles (dpn) size 5 US (8 UK, 4mm) *or size needed to obtain gauge.*

Size 5 circular needle 20 or 26" <51 or 66cm> long

Three 3/8" <1cm> pearl half-round buttons

1.25"-wide <3cm> plaid taffeta ribbon for bows

40 (40, 40, 40, 60, 80)" <101.5 (101.5, 101.5, 101.5, 152, 203) cm> OR 10" <25.5cm> for each bow

Stitch holders

Crochet hook

The box pleats in this cotton party dress are really very simple. Cast-off stitches for the pleat are held in back of the work and sewn into the pleat after the bodice is complete. It couldn't be simpler, and the result is charming.

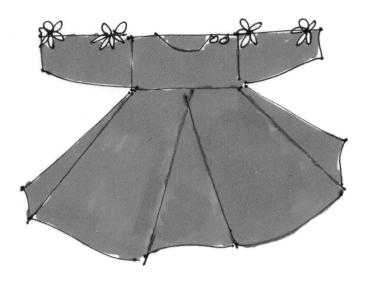

Gauge

22 sts and 28 rows = 4"
<10cm> in Stockinette st

*Always check gauge to save time
and ensure correct yardage!*

Skirt

With circular needle, cast on
184 (188, 196, 204, 220, 236)
sts. Join, taking care not to
twist sts on needle. Place marker for beg of rnd. (K1 rnd, p 1
rnd) twice for hem. Work pleats
as foll: *K20 (21, 23, 25, 29,
33), sl 1 knitwise, k24, sl 1 knitwise; rep from * around. K 1
rnd. Rep last 2 rnds for a total
of 7.5 (8, 9, 10, 12, 14)" <19
(20.5, 23, 25.5, 30.5, 35.5)
cm> above hem. Next rnd:
*K20 (21, 23, 25, 29, 33), bind
off next 26 sts for box pleat;

rep from * around. K next rnd,
leaving bound-off sts for pleats
at back of work.80 (84, 92,
100, 116, 132) sts. K 2 rnds.

Front Bodice

Divide work in half for front and
back bodice. Place back sts on
a holder and work in St st (k on
RS, p on WS) on front sts with
straight needles for 2.5 (2.5,
2.5, 3, 4, 6)" <6.5 (6.5, 6.5,
7.5, 10, 15) cm>, end with a
WS row. Neck shaping: Work 16
(16, 17, 18, 21, 24) sts, join
2nd skein of yarn and bind off
center 8 (10, 12, 14, 16, 18)
sts for neck, work to end.
Working both sides at the same
time, dec 1 st at each neck
edge every other row 5
times.11 (11, 12, 13, 16, 19)
sts each side. Work 0 (0, 4, 4,

4, 4) rows even. On next (WS)
row, work buttonholes on left
front shoulder as foll: P1 (1, 1, 2,
3, 3), *yo, p2tog, p2 (2, 2, 2, 3,
4); rep from * once more, yo, p2
tog, p to end. Work 2 rows even.
Bind off left shoulder sts. Place
right shoulder sts on a holder.

Back Bodice

Work as for front, omitting neck
shaping and buttonholes. On last
(RS) row, work 11 (11, 12, 13, 16,
19) sts and place on a holder for
right shoulder, work next 18 (20,
22, 24, 26, 28) sts and place on a
2nd holder for back neck, work to
end. Working on left shoulder sts
only, k next row on WS for turning
ridge. Cont in St st for 6 rows for
button placket. Bind off.

Sleeves

Slip shoulder sts from holder to
two straight needles. *With WS tog
and a third straight needle, k the
first st on front needle tog with
first st on back needle, *k next st
on front and back needles tog, sl
the first st over 2nd st to bind
off; rep from * until all sts are
bound off. Fold turning ridge of
left back shoulder to WS and tack
side of placket along back shoulder edge, then tack 1 st of front
and back tog at shoulder edge.

Place markers on front and back 4
(4.25, 4.25, 4.5, 5, 6)" <10 (11,
11, 11.5, 12.5, 15) cm> down

from shoulder seams for armholes. With RS facing and dpn, pick up and k44 (46, 46, 50, 56, 68) sts between markers. Join and place marker at underarm. Work in St st (k every rnd) for 6 rnds. Dec 1 st each end of next rnd (by knitting 2 tog before and after marker), then every 4th row 6 (8, 6, 6, 0, 11) times more, then every 2nd (0, 6th, 6th, 6th, 6th) row 2 (0, 2, 3, 9, 4) times 26 (28, 28, 30, 36, 36) sts. Work even until sleeve measures 5 (5.5, 6, 7, 8.5, 10.5)" <12.5 (14, 15, 18, 21.5, 26.5) cm>. P next rnd for turning ridge. Cont St st for 5 rnds more. Place sts on a strand of yarn for later finishing.

Finishing

Neckband: With RS facing and straight needles, beg at left front shoulder, pick up and k54 (56, 60, 64, 68, 72) sts evenly around neck edge, including sts from holders. K 2 rows, then bind off.

Fold pleats evenly to inside of fabric and sew in place. Sew buttons to button placket. Fold 5 rows at lower edge of sleeve to WS at turning ridge and sew live sts in place. With crochet hook,

pull ribbon through two sts on top sleeve ridge and tie bows, beg just below shoulder seam, placing 2 (2, 2, 2, 3, 4) bows, with one at shoulder and cuff and 0 (0, 0, 0, 1, 2) spaced evenly between.

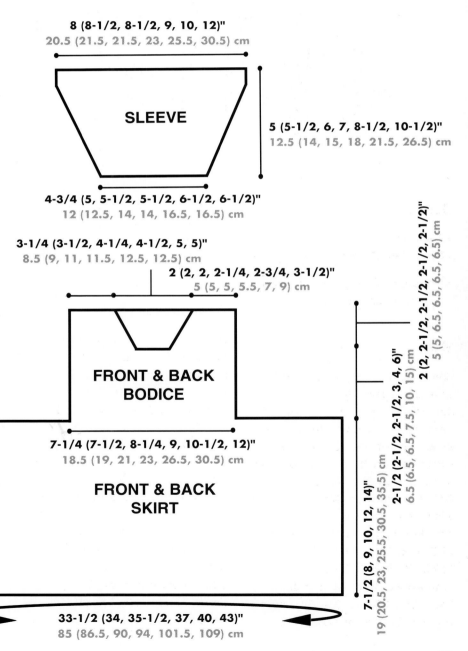

8 (8-1/2, 8-1/2, 9, 10, 12)"
20.5 (21.5, 21.5, 23, 25.5, 30.5) cm

SLEEVE

5 (5-1/2, 6, 7, 8-1/2, 10-1/2)"
12.5 (14, 15, 18, 21.5, 26.5) cm

4-3/4 (5, 5-1/2, 5-1/2, 6-1/2, 6-1/2)"
12 (12.5, 14, 14, 16.5, 16.5) cm

3-1/4 (3-1/2, 4-1/4, 4-1/2, 5, 5)"
8.5 (9, 11, 11.5, 12.5, 12.5) cm

2 (2, 2, 2-1/4, 2-3/4, 3-1/2)"
5 (5, 5, 5.5, 7, 9) cm

FRONT & BACK BODICE

7-1/4 (7-1/2, 8-1/4, 9, 10-1/2, 12)"
18.5 (19, 21, 23, 26.5, 30.5) cm

FRONT & BACK SKIRT

2 (2, 2-1/2, 2-1/2, 2-1/2, 2-1/2)"
5 (5, 6.5, 6.5, 6.5, 6.5) cm

2-1/2 (2-1/2, 2-1/2, 3, 4, 6)"
6.5 (6.5, 6.5, 7.5, 10, 15) cm

7-1/2 (8, 9, 10, 12, 14)"
19 (20.5, 23, 25.5, 30.5, 35.5) cm

33-1/2 (34, 35-1/2, 37, 40, 43)"
85 (86.5, 90, 94, 101.5, 109) cm

THE GREAT OUTDOORS

Children love to play outdoors, and warm, soft hand-knits are cozy and comfortable. Terrific in cool cottons, blends, or the warmest wools, these sweaters are sporting for a breezy day at the beach or a chilly romp in the snow—perfect for running, doing cartwheels, or playing tag in any weather.

Red Riding Hood

Sizes

To fit 2 (4, 6) years

Finished chest, (closed):
25 (30, 32)"
<63.5 (76, 81) cm>

Length, shoulder to hem:
12 (14, 16)"
<30.5 (35.5, 40.5) cm>

Materials

A superwash, worsted weight wool yarn that will obtain gauge given below. A bulky looped mohair for trim

550 (700, 900) yards <495 (630, 810) meters> MC

100 yards <90 meters> CC

Knitting needles size 10 US (4 UK, 6mm), and double pointed needles (dpn), size 10 *or size needed to obtain gauge*

Stitch holders and markers

Separating zipper 12 (14, 16)" <30.5 (35.5, 40.5) cm> long

Sample in photograph knit in Classic Elite Stonington, #9158 Red (MC) and Mouton Mohair #4613 Black

Gauge

14 sts and 24 rows = 4" <10cm> over Seed st

Always check gauge to save time and ensure correct yardage!

The wolf would be stopped in his tracks by this little hooded jacket! The seed stitch pattern gives the fabric a strong, supple hand, and the jacket is cozy and fetching with faux mouton hood and sleeve trim.

Pattern Stitch

Seed St

Row 1 (RS): *K1, p1; rep from *
to end.

Row 2: K the purl sts and p the
knit sts.

Rep row 2 for Seed st.

Back

With MC, cast on 44 (52, 56)
sts. Work in Garter st (k every
row) for 4 rows. Cont in Seed st
until piece measures 12 (14,
16)" <30.5 (35.5, 40.5) cm>
from beg, end with a WS row.
On next row, work 13 (16, 18)

sts and place on a holder for
later finishing, place next 18
(20, 20) sts on a 2nd holder for
back neck, place rem 13 (16,
18) sts on a 3rd holder for later
finishing.

Left Front

Cast on 22 (26, 28) sts and
work as for back until same
length as back. On next RS row,
place 13 (16, 18) sts on a holder for shoulder and place rem 9
(10, 10) sts on a 2nd holder for
hood.

Right Front

Work as for left front, reversing
sts on holder.

Sleeves

With wrong sides facing and MC,
place sts for both right shoulders
on two parallel dpn. With a third
dpn, k through first st on each
needle, then the 2nd, and pass
first over 2nd to bind off. Cont in
this way to end for a knitted
seam. Work in same way on left
shoulder. With RS facing and MC,
mark for sleeves 6 (6.5, 7)" <15
(16.5, 17.5) cm> down from
shoulder seam. With RS facing,

pick up and k42 (46, 50) sts between markers. Work in Seed st for 5 rows. Cont in Seed st, dec 1 st each end of next row, then every 6th row 4 (5, 8) times more, every 4th row 3 (3, 1) times. Work even on rem 26 (28, 30) sts until sleeve measures 7.5 (8.5, 10)" <19 (21.5, 25.5) cm>. Bind off loosely and evenly.

Sleeve trim

With RS facing and CC, pick up 26 (28, 30) sts along bound-off edge of sleeve and work in Stockinette st for 4 rows. Bind off loosely and evenly.

Hood

With RS facing, sl sts from holders to needle as foll: 9 (10, 10) sts on right front, 18 (20, 20) sts on back neck, 9 (10, 10) sts on left front, to 36 (40, 40) sts. With MC, work in Seed st for 6.5 (7, 7.5)" <16.5 (17.5, 18) cm>. Divide sts on 2 dpn. Knit seam as for shoulder seams.

Hood trim

With RS facing and CC, pick up 48 (52, 52) sts around hood opening. Work in Stockinette st for 4 rows. Bind off loosely and evenly.

Finishing

Weave in all loose ends.
Sew sleeve and side seams.
Sew in zipper.

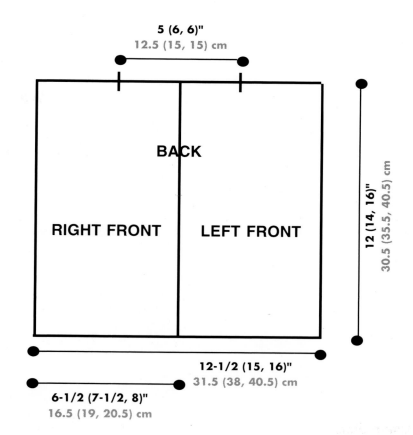

5 (6, 6)"
12.5 (15, 15) cm

BACK

RIGHT FRONT   LEFT FRONT

12 (14, 16)"
30.5 (35.5, 40.5) cm

12-1/2 (15, 16)"
31.5 (38, 40.5) cm

6-1/2 (7-1/2, 8)"
16.5 (19, 20.5) cm

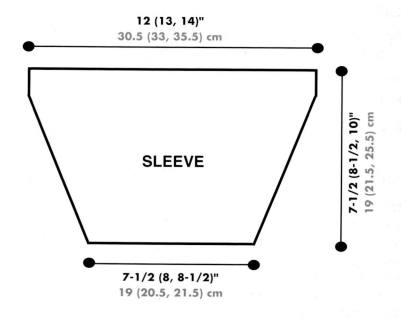

12 (13, 14)"
30.5 (33, 35.5) cm

SLEEVE

7-1/2 (8-1/2, 10)"
19 (21.5, 25.5) cm

7-1/2 (8, 8-1/2)"
19 (20.5, 21.5) cm

Ski, Baby!

Sizes

To fit 3 months
(6 months, 1 year, 2 years)

Finished chest:
19.5 (21, 22, 24)"
<49.5 (53.5, 56, 61) cm>

Materials

DK weight wool/cotton blend that
will obtain gauge given below

410 (470, 560, 690) yards
<370 (425, 504, 622) meters>
MC, 125 yards <112 meters>
each color A and color B

Knitting needles size 4 US (9
UK, 3.50 mm) *or size needed to
obtain gauge.* 1 set (5) double
pointed needles (dpn), size 4;
20" <51cm> circular needle
sizes 3 and 4 (10 and 9 UK,
3.25 and 3.50mm).

Crochet hook size F US (9 UK,
3.5mm) for Helmet

Ten .5" <1.5cm> buttons

Stitch holders and stitch
markers

Sample in photograph knit in Stahl
Olé, Forest #S635 (MC), Aqua #S610
(A) and Raspberry #S623 (B)

*A one-piece
jumpsuit keeps
tiny tots toasty
outdoors,
whether in a
backpack or
sling. Buttons
make changing
a snap, and the
snowflakes add
a twinkling,
easy-to-knit
detail. The
helmet keeps
little ears cov-
ered and snug.*

Gauge

22 sts and 28 rows = 4"
<10cm> in Stockinette st.

*Always check gauge to save time
and ensure correct yardage!*

JUMPSUIT

Left Leg

With straight needles and A, cast
on 54 (60, 66, 72) sts. Cut A,
join MC and k 1 row on RS.
Work in k1, p1 rib for 6 (6, 6, 8)
rows. Next row (WS): Rib 5 sts, p
to last 5 sts, rib 5. Next (buttonhole) row (RS): Rib 5, k to last 5
sts, yo, k2 tog, (buttonhole), rib
3. Cont to work buttonhole
every 12 (14, 15, 16) rows twice
more, keeping first and last 5
sts in rib and rem sts in St st (k
on RS, p on WS) and chart pat,
AT THE SAME TIME, inc 1 st
each end (working inc sts inside
of rib sts and into chart pat)
every 4th row 6 (8, 9, 8) times,
then every 2nd (2nd, 6th, 6th)
row 4 (2, 1, 3) times—74 (80,
86, 94) sts. Work even until 38
(42, 50, 56) rows have been
worked above rib—piece measures approx 6.5 (7, 8, 9.5)"
<16.5 (18, 20.5, 24) cm> from
beg, end with a WS row.

Crotch shaping

Bind off 5 (6, 7, 8) sts at beg of
next 2 rows, dec 1 st at each
end of next 10 (10, 12, 12)
rows—54 (58, 60, 66) sts. Place
sts on a holder.

Right Leg

Work as for left leg, working buttonholes at beg of RS rows as foll: Rib 3, yo, k2 tog, work to end.

Body

With RS of both legs facing, sl sts of right leg to larger circular needle, place marker for beg of rnd (center back), sl sts of left leg to holder. Cont to work St st and chart pat in rnds (k every rnd), dec 0 (1, 0, 0) st at beg and end of rnd—108 (114, 120, 132) sts. Work even in pat until piece measures 10.5 (11, 12.5, 14)" <26.5 (28, 31.5, 35.5) cm> from beg. Change to smaller circular needle.

Waistband

*K1 MC, k1 A; rep from * around. Rep last rnd 7 times more.

Divide for front and back

Sl first 27 (28, 30, 33) sts and last 27 (29, 30, 33) sts to straight needles, place rem 54 (57, 60, 66) sts on a holder for front. Beg with a RS row, cont in St st and chart pat (working back and forth) on back sts for 5 (5.5, 6, 6.5)" <12.5 (14, 15, 16.5) cm> above waistband. Cut MC and B. Join A and p next row on WS. On next row, place first 19 (20, 21, 23) sts on a holder for right shoulder, place next 16 (17, 18, 20) sts on

another holder for back neck, p rem 19 (20, 21, 23) sts for turning ridge. Cut A, join MC and cont in St st for 7 rows for button placket. Bind off.

Front

Sl 54 (57, 60, 66) sts from front holder to straight needles and work as for back for 3 (3.5, 4, 4.5)" <7.5 (9, 10, 11.5) cm> above waistband.

Neck shaping

Work 23 (24, 25, 27) sts, join 2nd ball of yarn and bind off center 8 (9, 10, 12) sts for neck, work to end. Working both sides at same time, dec 1 st at neck edge every other row 4 times—19 (20, 21, 23) sts each side. Work even for 4.5 (5, 5.5, 6)" <11.5 (12.5, 14, 15) cm> above waistband. On next (WS) row, work buttonholes on left front shoulder as foll: P3 (4, 3, 3), *yo, p2 tog, p3 (3, 4, 5); rep from * once more, yo, p2 tog, p to end. K 1 row. Cut MC. Join A and p next row. Bind off left shoulder sts. Place right shoulder sts on a holder.

Sleeves

Slip shoulder sts from holder to two straight needles. *With WS facing* and a third straight needle, k the first st on front needle tog with first st on back

needle, *k next st on front and back needles tog, sl the first st over 2nd st to bind off; rep from * until all sts are bound off. Fold turning ridge of left back shoulder to WS and tack side of placket along back shoulder edge, then tack 1 st of front and back tog at shoulder edge. Place markers on front and back 5 (5.5, 6, 6.5)" <12.5 (14, 15, 16.5) cm> down from shoulder seams for armholes. With RS facing, straight needles, and MC, pick up and k54 (60, 66, 72) sts between markers. Work in St st and chart pat for 4 rows. Dec 1 st each end of next row, then every 4th row 3 (3, 3, 4) times more, then every other row 7 (9, 11, 12) times—32 (34, 36, 38) sts. Work even for 5 (5.5, 6, 7)" <12.5 (14, 15, 18) cm> from pick-up row. Work in k1, p1 rib with MC for 4 (4, 6, 6) rows. With A, bind off loosely in rib.

Finishing

Neckband

With *RS facing*, straight needles, and A, pick up and k59 (61, 63, 67) sts evenly around neck edge. Work in k1, p1 rib for 2 rows. Work a buttonhole in 3rd from last st on next row. Rib 3 rows more. Bind off in rib. Sew on buttons.

Helmet

Change to dpn and divide sts evenly over 4 needles as foll: place sts of one earflap on needle, cast on 30 (34, 38) sts for back, place sts of 2nd earflap on needle, cast on 42 (46, 50) sts for front. Join, taking care not to twist sts on needles—120 (132, 144) sts. Work in k1, p1 rib for 3 (3.5, 4)" <7.5 (9, 10) cm> more. P 1 rnd. Join MC and cont work in St st (k every rnd) and chart pat, as foll: Work 2 rnds even. Next rnd: *K8 (9, 10), k2 tog; rep from * around—108 (120, 132) sts. Work 1 rnd even. Next rnd: *K7 (8, 9), k2 tog; rep from * around—96 (108, 120) sts. Work 1 rnd even. Cont in this way to dec 12 sts every other rnd, working 1 less st between decs every dec rnd, until there are 6 sts. Join B and work on these 6 sts for topknot for 2.5 (3.25, 3.5)" <6.5 (8.5, 9) cm>. Fasten off. Draw through sts, pull tog tightly and secure.

Finishing

With *RS facing*, crochet hook, and A, work picot edge around lower edge of helmet and earflaps as foll: *sc in next 2 sts, 3 sc in next st; rep from * around. Make two 9 (9, 10)" <23 (23, 25.5) cm> chains and attach to end of each earflap.

HELMET

Helmet with earflaps, snowflakes, and topknot.

Sizes

To fit Small/3-6 months (Medium/1 year, Large/2 years)

Finished circumference 16 (17, 18)" <40.5 (43, 45.5) cm>

Gauge

34 sts and 28 rows = 4" <10cm> in k1, p1 rib.

Earflaps (make 2)

With straight needles and A, cast on 3 sts. Work in k1, p1 rib, inc 1 st each end *every* row until there are 24 (26, 28) sts. Work even for 20 (22, 24) rows or 2.75 (3, 3.5)" <7 (7.5, 9) cm> from beg.

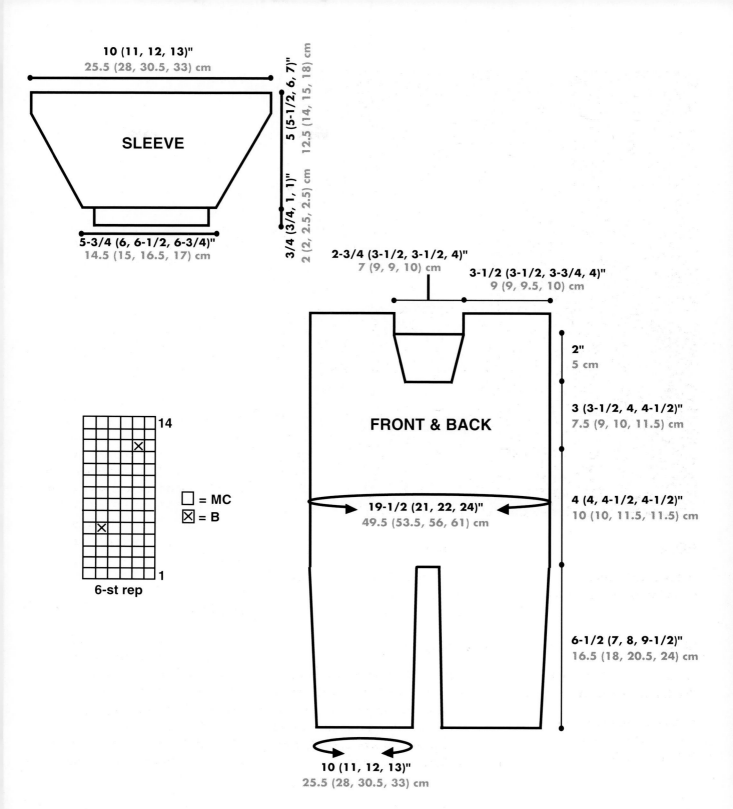

10 (11, 12, 13)"
25.5 (28, 30.5, 33) cm

SLEEVE

5 (5-1/2, 6, 7)"
12.5 (14, 15, 18) cm

3/4 (3/4, 1, 1)"
2 (2, 2.5, 2.5) cm

5-3/4 (6, 6-1/2, 6-3/4)"
14.5 (15, 16.5, 17) cm

2-3/4 (3-1/2, 3-1/2, 4)"
7 (9, 9, 10) cm

3-1/2 (3-1/2, 3-3/4, 4)"
9 (9, 9.5, 10) cm

2"
5 cm

FRONT & BACK

3 (3-1/2, 4, 4-1/2)"
7.5 (9, 10, 11.5) cm

19-1/2 (21, 22, 24)"
49.5 (53.5, 56, 61) cm

4 (4, 4-1/2, 4-1/2)"
10 (10, 11.5, 11.5) cm

6-1/2 (7, 8, 9-1/2)"
16.5 (18, 20.5, 24) cm

□ = MC
⊠ = B

14

1

6-st rep

10 (11, 12, 13)"
25.5 (28, 30.5, 33) cm

Skating

Sizes

To fit 1 year (2 years, 4 years, 6 years)

Finished chest, sweater:
25 (26, 28, 30)"
<63.5 (66, 71, 76) cm>

Length, shoulder to hem, sweater:
9.5 (10, 11.5, 13)"
<24 (25.5, 29, 33) cm>

Finished waist, skirt:
18.5 (20.5, 22.5, 24.5)"
<47 (52, 57, 62) cm>

Materials

For Sweater and Hat:

Worsted weight wool that will obtain gauge given below

445 (550, 650, 720) yards
<400 (495, 585, 650) meters>

For Skirt:

210 (280, 400, 590) yards
<190 (252, 360, 530) meters>

Knitting needles sizes 4 US (9 UK, 3.50mm) and 6 US (7 UK, 4.5mm) *or size needed to obtain gauge*

Size 6 circular needle 20" <51cm> long (for skirt)

Four .5" <1.5cm> buttons (for sweater), 6 (6, 7, 7) .5" <1.5cm> buttons (for skirt)

Stitch holders

Cable needle (cn)

The full skirt of this three-piece set is easily worked up in worsted weight wool, with even increases all around after the waist cable work. Topped off with the beret and the cropped sweater, the skirt twirls prettily on your little skater!

Gauge

18 sts and 24 rows = 4" <10 cm> in Stockinette st using larger needles.

Always check gauge to save time and ensure correct yardage!

Cable Pat (over 4 sts)

Row 1 (RS): K4.

Rows 2 and 4: P4.

Row 3: Sl 2 sts to cn and hold in back of work, k2, k2 from cn.

Rep rows 1-4 for cable pat.

SWEATER

Back

With smaller needles, cast on 57 (59, 63, 68) sts. Work in k1, p1 rib for 4 (4, 6, 8) rows. Change to larger needles and work in St st (k on RS, p on WS) until piece measures 6.5 (7, 8, 9)" <16.5 (18, 20.5, 23) cm> from beg. P next row on WS, inc 12 (14, 14, 16) sts evenly across—69 (73, 77, 84) sts. Beg cable and rib yoke: Next row (RS): P1, (k1, p1) 2 (3, 4, 3) times, *work cable over next 4 sts, p1, (k1, p1) 3 times; rep from * 4 (4, 4, 5) times more, work cable over 4 sts, p1, (k1, p1) 2 (3, 4, 3)

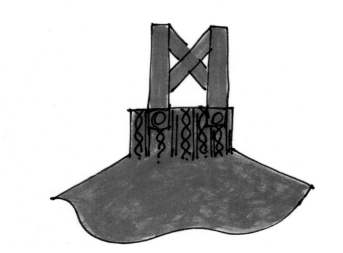

times. Cont in pats as established, working sts between cables in k1, p1 rib, until piece measures 9.5 (10, 11.5, 13)" <24 (25.5, 29, 33) cm> from beg. On next (RS) row, work 23 (24, 25, 27) sts and place on a holder for right shoulder, work next 23 (25, 27, 30) sts and place on a 2nd holder for back neck, work to end. Working on left shoulder sts only, k next row on WS for turning ridge. Cont in St st for 6 rows for button placket. Bind off.

Front

Work as for back until 10 (10, 10, 14) rows have been worked in yoke pat.

Neck Shaping: Work 27 (28, 30, 32) sts, join 2nd ball of yarn and bind off center 15 (17, 17, 20) sts for neck, work to end. Working both sides at same time, dec 1 st at neck edge every other row 4 (4, 5, 5) times, AT THE SAME TIME, when piece measures 3 rows less than back to right shoulder, work 3 buttonholes evenly spaced across left shoulder by yo, p2 tog for each buttonhole. Work 2 rows even. Bind off left shoulder sts. Place right shoulder sts on a holder.

Sleeves

Slip shoulder sts from holder to two straight needles. *With WS facing* and a third straight needle, k the first st on front needle tog with first st on back needle, *k next st on front and back needles tog, sl the first st over 2nd st to bind off; rep from * until all sts are bound off. Fold turning ridge of left back shoulder to WS and tack side of placket along back shoulder edge, then tack 1 st of front and back tog at shoulder edge. Place markers on front and back 5 (5.5, 6, 7)" <12.5 (14, 15, 18) cm> down from shoulder seams for armholes. With RS facing, larger needles, and MC, pick up and k46 (52, 56, 64) sts between markers. Next row (WS): P20 (23, 25, 29), k1, p4 (cable sts), k1, p20 (23, 25, 29). Cont in pat as established for 4 rows more. Dec 1 st each end of next row, then every 6th row 3 (1, 5, 4) times more, then every 4th row 5 (9, 5, 8) times—28 (30, 34, 38) sts. Work until 7.5 (8.25, 9.5, 10.5)" <19 (21, 24, 26.5) cm> from pick-up row. Work in k1, p1 rib for 4 (4, 6, 8) rows. Bind off in rib.

Finishing

Neckband: With RS facing and smaller needles, beg at left front shoulder, pick up and k67 (73, 79, 89) sts evenly around neck edge, including sts from holders. Work in k1, p1 rib for 2 (3, 5, 5) rows. On next row, work a buttonhole at 3 sts from front edge. Rib 2 (3, 5, 5) rows more. Bind off in rib. Sew side and sleeve seams. Sew on buttons.

SKIRT

Ribbed high-waisted bodice: With smaller straight needles, cast on 105 (116, 127, 138) sts. Beg cable and rib yoke: Next row (RS): K3, *p1, (k1, p1) 3 times, work cable over next 4 sts; rep from * 8 (9, 10, 11) times more, k3. Cont in pats as established, working first and last 3 sts in Garter st (k every row) and sts between cables in k1, p1 rib, for 2.75 (3.25, 4.25, 6)" <7 (8.5, 10.5, 15) cm> from beg, AT THE SAME TIME, work 2 (2, 3, 3) buttonholes in Garter st at beg of RS rows, by k1, yo, k2 tog, with the first one at .5" <1.5cm> from beg and the next 1 (1, 2, 2) spaced 1.5 (2.5, 1.5, 2.5)" <4 (6.5, 4, 6.5) cm> apart.

Circle skirt

Change to larger circular needle. Bind off first 3 sts, k to end, dec 0 (2, 1, 0) sts—102 (111, 123, 135) sts. Join, place marker for beg of rnd. Cont in St st (k every rnd) as foll: k 1 rnd. Next (inc) rnd (RS): *K2, inc 1 st in next st; rep from * around—136 (148, 164, 180) sts. K 1 rnd. Next (inc) rnd (RS): *K3, inc 1 st in next st; rep from * around—170 (185, 205, 225) sts. K 1 rnd. Cont to inc 34 (37, 41, 45) sts every other rnd, working 1 more st between inc every inc rnd, until there are 238 (259, 328, 350) sts. Work even in St st until 4.25 (5, 5.5, 6)" <10.5 (12.5, 14, 15) cm> have been worked above yoke. (K 1 rnd, p 1 rnd) twice for hem. Bind off firmly.

Finishing

Sew buttons on Garter st band opposite buttonholes. Sew 2 more buttons on inside back waist and outside front waist for straps, centering over cables, .75" <2cm> from the top.

Straps

With smaller needles, cast on 8 (8, 10, 10) sts. Row 1: K1 (1, 2, 2), p1, k4 (for cable), p1, k1 (1, 2, 2). Row 2: K1 (1, 2, 2), k1, p4 (for cable), k1, k1 (1, 2, 2). Row 3: Work 3 (3, 4, 4) sts, yo,

k2 tog (buttonhole), work to end. Cont in pats as established for 14 (15, 17, 19)" <35.5 (38, 43, 48.5) cm>. Make a buttonhole as before. Work 2 rows. Bind off.

BERET

Sizes

To fit Small/1 year (Medium/2-4 years, Large/6 years)

Finished circumference: 16 (18, 19.5)" <40.5 (45.5 49.5) cm>

With smaller needles, cast on 90 (100, 110) sts. Work in k1, p1 rib for 6 rows, inc 30 (34, 31) sts evenly across last row—120 (134, 141) sts. Change to larger needles. Beg cable and rib yoke: Next row (RS): P1, *work cable over next 4 sts, p1, k1, p1; rep from * to end. Cont

in pat as established for 4 (5.5, 7)" <10 (14, 18) cm>. Next row: P1, *work 4 sts, k2 tog, p1; rep from * to end—103 (115, 121) sts. Work 1 row even. Next row: P1 *work 4 sts, k2 tog; rep from * to end—86 (96, 101) sts. Cont to dec 17 (19, 20) sts every other row, working 1 less st between dec every dec row, until there are 18 (20, 21) sts. K2 tog on next 2 rows. Fasten off, leaving an end for sewing. Draw through sts, pull tog tightly and secure. Sew back seam.

Pom-pom

Wrap 15 yards <15 meters> around a 2.25" <5.5cm> cardboard rectangle. Remove cardboard and wrap a 12" <30.5cm> length of yarn around center. Cut through loops on both ends, fluff and trim evenly. Sew firmly to top of beret.

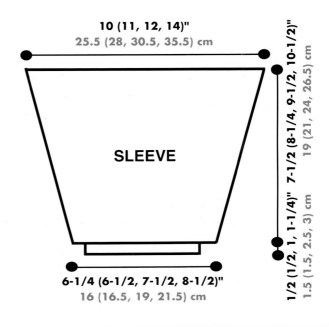

10 (11, 12, 14)"
25.5 (28, 30.5, 35.5) cm

SLEEVE

6-1/4 (6-1/2, 7-1/2, 8-1/2)"
16 (16.5, 19, 21.5) cm

1/2 (1/2, 1, 1-1/4)" 7-1/2 (8-1/4, 9-1/2, 10-1/2)"
1.5 (1.5, 2.5, 3) cm 19 (21, 24, 26.5) cm

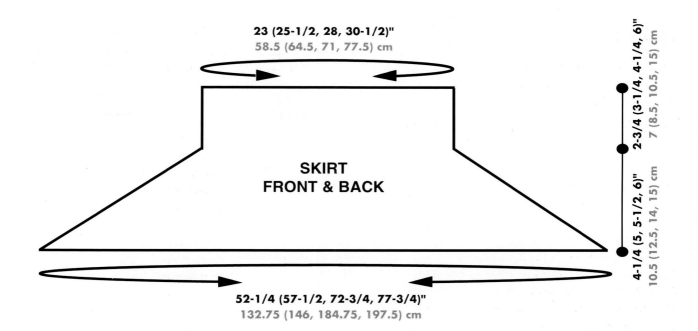

23 (25-1/2, 28, 30-1/2)"
58.5 (64.5, 71, 77.5) cm

**SKIRT
FRONT & BACK**

2-3/4 (3-1/4, 4-1/4, 6)"
7 (8.5, 10.5, 15) cm

4-1/4 (5, 5-1/2, 6)"
10.5 (12.5, 14, 15) cm

52-1/4 (57-1/2, 72-3/4, 77-3/4)"
132.75 (146, 184.75, 197.5) cm

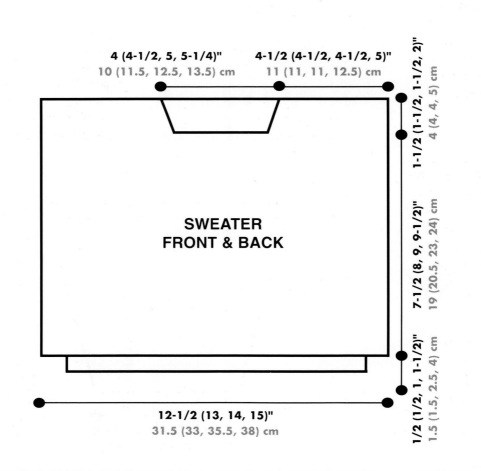

4 (4-1/2, 5, 5-1/4)"
10 (11.5, 12.5, 13.5) cm

4-1/2 (4-1/2, 4-1/2, 5)"
11 (11, 11, 12.5) cm

1-1/2 (1-1/2, 1-1/2, 2)"
4 (4, 4, 5) cm

**SWEATER
FRONT & BACK**

1-1/2 (1-1/2, 1, 1-1/2)"
4 (4, 2.5, 4) cm

7-1/2 (8, 9, 9-1/2)"
19 (20.5, 23, 24) cm

1/2 (1/2, 1, 1-1/2)"
1.5 (1.5, 2.5, 4) cm

12-1/2 (13, 14, 15)"
31.5 (33, 35.5, 38) cm

Faux Fisherman

Sizes

To fit 2 (4, 6, 8, 10) years

Finished chest, sweater:
25 (28, 30, 32, 34)"
<63.5 (71, 76, 81, 86.5) cm>

Length, shoulder to hem:
13 (16, 17.5, 19, 20.5)"
<33 (40.5, 44.5, 48, 52) cm>

Materials

Heavy worsted weight wool that
will obtain gauge given below

500 (660, 800, 900, 1050)
yards <450 (594, 720, 810,
945) meters>

Knitting needles sizes 8 and 10
US (5 and 4 UK, 5.5 and 6mm)
or size needed to obtain gauge.
Size 8 circular needle 16 or 29"
<40 or 80 cm> long. Size 10
double pointed needles (dpn)

Stitch holders and markers

Cable needle (cn)

Sample in photograph knit in Cynthia
Helene Merino Chunky in #173 Denim
or #9501 Natural

*Originally
designed for my
son, Alexander,
this sweater got
rave reviews
wherever he
went. Although
it has the look
and feel of a
classic, tricky-to-
knit Irish fisher-
man's sweater,
it is actually
quick and easy
with #10
needles and
a washable,
bulky yarn.*

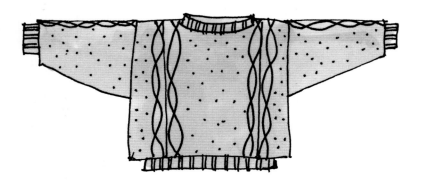

Gauge

14 sts and 22 rows = 4"
<10cm> over Seed st using
larger needles

19 sts cable panel = 3.25"
<8cm> using larger needles

*Always check gauge to save time
and ensure correct yardage!*

Pattern Stitches

Seed St

Row 1: *K1, p1; rep from *.

Row 2: K the purl sts and p the
knit sts.

Rep row 2 for Seed st.

Left Twist—LT (over 2 sts)

Row 1: (RS) K 2nd st on LH
needle *behind* first st, then k
first st, drop both sts from
needle.

Row 2: P2.

Rep rows 1 and 2 for LT.

4-ST (6-ST) Cable

Rows 1 and 3: (RS) K4 (6).

Row 2 and all WS rows: P4 (6).

Row 5: Sl 2 sts to cn and hold
to *back* of work, k2, k2 from cn
(sl 3 sts to cn and hold to *back*
of work, k3, k3 from cn).

Row 7: Rep row 1.

Row 8: Rep row 2.

Rep rows 1-8 for 4-st (6-st)
cable.

Back

With smaller needles, cast on 45
(51, 55, 57, 61) sts. Work in k1,
p1 rib for 1 (1, 1.5, 1.5, 1.5)"
<2.5 (2.5, 4, 4, 4) cm>, inc 14
(15, 15, 16, 16) sts evenly across
last WS row to 59 (66, 70, 73,
77) sts. Change to larger needles.
Establish cable pat—Next row
(RS): Work 3 (4, 6, 7, 8) sts in
Seed st, *p1, LT over 2 sts, p1*,
4-st cable, rep between *'s, 6-st
cable, p1, 15 (20, 20, 21, 23) sts
Seed st, p1, 6-st cable, rep
between *'s, 4-st cable, rep
between *'s, 3 (4, 6, 7, 8) sts in
Seed st. Cont in pats as established until piece measures 13
(16, 17.5, 19, 20.5)" <33 (40.5,
44.5, 48, 52) cm> from beg.
Place 20 (23, 24, 25, 26) sts on a
holder for one shoulder, place
next 19 (20, 22, 23, 25) sts on a
2nd holder for back neck, place
rem 20 (23, 24, 25, 26) sts on a
3rd holder for other shoulder.

Front

Work as for back until piece
measures 11 (13.5, 15, 16.5,
18)" <28 (34, 38, 42, 45.5) cm>
from beg. Work neck shaping as
foll: Next RS row, work 26 (29,
31, 32, 33) sts, join 2nd ball of
yarn and bind off center 7 (8, 8,
9, 11) sts, work to end.
Working both sides at same
time, bind off from each neck
edge 2 sts twice, 1 st 2 (2, 3, 3,
3) times. Work even until same
length as back. Place rem 20
(23, 24, 25, 26) sts each side
on holders for later finishing.

Sleeves

With wrong sides facing, place
sts for both right shoulders on
two parallel dpn. With a third
dpn, k through first st on each
needle, then the 2nd, and pass
first over 2nd to bind off. Cont

in this way to end for a knitted seam. Work in same way for left shoulder seam. With RS facing, mark for sleeves 6 (6.5, 7, 7.5, 8)" <15.5 (16.5, 18, 19, 20.5) cm> down from shoulder seam. With RS facing, pick up and k46 (50, 54, 58, 60) sts between markers. Establish cable pat—Next row (WS): Work 17 (19, 21, 23, 24) sts in Seed st, k1, row 2 of LT, k1, row 2 of 4-st cable, k1, row 2 of LT, k1, 17 (19, 21, 23, 24) sts in Seed st. Cont in pats as established for 4 rows more, then dec 1 st each end of next row, then every 4th row 9 (10, 11, 13, 13) times more. When sleeve measures 7.5 (10, 11, 12.5, 14)" <19 (25.5, 28, 32, 35.5) cm>, work 1 (1, 1.5, 1.5, 1.5)" <2.5 (2.5, 4, 4, 4) cm> in k1, p1 rib on rem 26 (28, 30, 30, 32) sts. Bind off loosely and evenly in rib.

Finishing

For neckband, with circular needle, k sts from back neck holder, pick up and k41 (42, 44, 45, 47) sts along front neck. Join and work in k1, p1 rib on 60 (62, 66, 68, 72) sts for 1" <2.5cm>. Bind off loosely in rib. Sew side and sleeve seams.

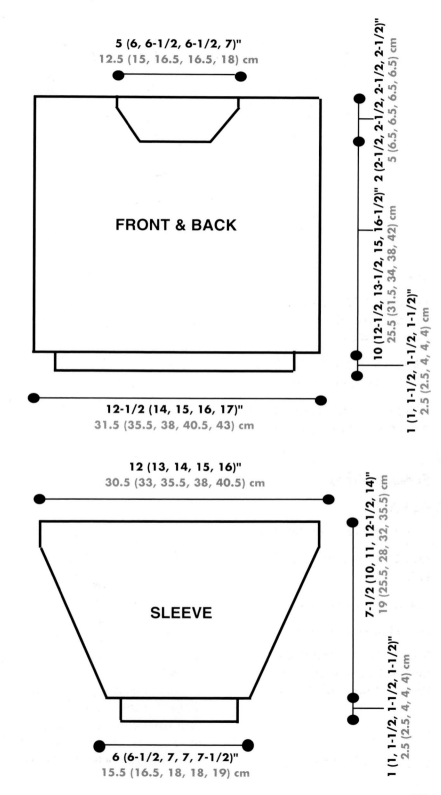

5 (6, 6-1/2, 6-1/2, 7)"
12.5 (15, 16.5, 16.5, 18) cm

FRONT & BACK

2 (2-1/2, 2-1/2, 2-1/2, 2-1/2)"
5 (6.5, 6.5, 6.5, 6.5) cm

10 (12-1/2, 13-1/2, 15, 16-1/2)"
25.5 (31.5, 34, 38, 42) cm

1 (1, 1-1/2, 1-1/2, 1-1/2)"
2.5 (2.5, 4, 4, 4) cm

12-1/2 (14, 15, 16, 17)"
31.5 (35.5, 38, 40.5, 43) cm

12 (13, 14, 15, 16)"
30.5 (33, 35.5, 38, 40.5) cm

SLEEVE

7-1/2 (10, 11, 12-1/2, 14)"
19 (25.5, 28, 32, 35.5) cm

1 (1, 1-1/2, 1-1/2, 1-1/2)"
2.5 (2.5, 4, 4, 4) cm

6 (6-1/2, 7, 7, 7-1/2)"
15.5 (16.5, 18, 18, 19) cm

Aran Ruffles

Sizes

To fit 6 months (1 year, 2 years, 4 years)

Finished chest:
19.5 (22, 25, 28)"
<49.5 (56, 63.5, 71) cm>

Length, shoulder to hem:
9 (10.5, 12.5, 15)"
<23 (26.5, 31.5, 38) cm>

Materials

For Sweater:

DK weight cotton that will obtain gauge given below

310 (410, 520, 690) yards
<280 (370, 468, 620) meters>

Knitting needles sizes 4 US (9 UK, 3.50mm) and 5 US (8 UK, 4mm) *or sizes needed to obtain gauge.*

Three .5" <1.5cm> buttons

Stitch holders

For Cap:

110 (125, 135, 140) yards

1 set (4) double pointed needles (dpn), sizes 4 and 5

Gauge

23 sts and 34 rows = 4"
<10cm> in chart pat using larger needles.

Always check gauge to save time and ensure correct yardage!

Pattern Stitch

K3, P1 RIB (multiple of 4 sts)

Row 1 (RS): *K3, p1; rep from * to end.

Row 2: K the knit sts and p the purl sts.

Rep row 2 for rib.

A simple diamond aran pattern is often used for traditional sweaters, but the ruffles ridging the neck and sleeves on this version are downright frisky. Seemingly complex, the companion hat is really quite simple; just make sure you turn your fabric after the turning ridge so the hat body is right-side-out!

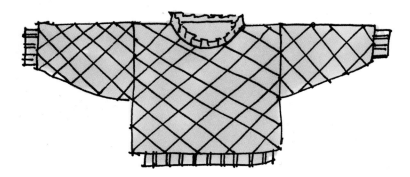

SWEATER

Back

With smaller needles, cast on 56 (60, 68, 76) sts. Work in k3, p1 rib for 1.5 (2, 2, 3)" <4 (5, 5, 7.5) cm>, end with a RS row. Change to larger needles and p next row on WS, inc 0 (4, 4, 4) sts evenly across—56 (64, 72, 80) sts. Cont in chart pat until 64 (72, 88, 104) rows of chart have been worked—piece measures approx 9 (10.5, 12.5, 15)" <23 (26.5, 31.5, 38) cm> from beg. On next (RS) row, work 15 (18, 20, 23) sts and place on a holder for right shoulder, work next 26 (28, 32, 34) sts and place on a 2nd holder for back neck, work to end. Working on left shoulder sts only, k next row on WS for turning ridge. Cont in St st (k on RS, p on WS) for 6 rows for button placket. Bind off.

Front

Work as for back until 56 (60, 76, 86) rows of chart have been worked—piece measures 8 (9, 11, 13)" <20.5 (23, 28, 33) cm> from beg.

Neck shaping

Work 19 (23, 26, 29) sts, join 2nd skein of yarn and bind off center 18 (18, 20, 22) sts for neck, work to end. Working both sides at same time, dec 1 st at neck edge every other row 4 (5, 6, 6) times—15 (18, 20, 23) sts each side. Work even until piece measures 3 rows less than back to right shoulder. On next (WS) row, work buttonholes on left front shoulder as foll: Work 2 sts, *yo, p2 tog, work 2 (3, 4, 6) sts; rep from * once more, yo, p2 tog, work to end. Work 2 rows even. Bind off left shoulder sts. Place right shoulder sts on a holder.

Sleeves

Slip shoulder sts from holder to two straight needles. *With WS facing* and a third straight needle, k the first st on front needle tog with first st on back needle, *k next st on front and back needles tog, sl the first st over 2nd st to bind off; rep from * until all sts are bound off. Fold turning ridge of left back shoulder to WS and tack side of placket along back shoulder edge, then tack 1 st of front and back tog at shoulder edge.

Place markers on front and back 4.25 (5, 5.5, 6.25)" <11 (12.5, 14, 16) cm> down from shoulder seams for armholes. With RS facing and larger needles, pick up and k48 (56, 64, 72) sts between markers. Work in chart pat for 8 rows. Dec 1 st each end of next row, then every 6th row 9 (4, 2, 0) times more, then every 4th row 0 (9, 13, 19) times—28 (28, 32, 32) sts. Work even until 64 (70, 74, 86) rows or 7.5 (8.25, 8.75, 10)" <19 (20.5, 21.5, 25.5) cm> have been worked from pick-up row. Work in k3, p1 rib for 4 (4, 6, 8) rows. On next row, inc 1 st in each st for ruffle—56 (56, 64, 64) sts. Cont in k4, p4 rib for 3 rows. Bind off firmly.

Finishing

Neckband: With RS facing and smaller needles, beg at left front shoulder, pick up and k60 (64, 72, 76) sts evenly around neck edge, including sts from holders. Work in k3, p1 rib for 4 (6, 8, 8) rows. Inc 1 st in each st on next row—120 (128, 144, 152) sts. Cont in k4, p4 rib for

3 rows. Bind off firmly. Sew side and sleeve seams. Sew on buttons.

RUFFLED ARAN CAP

Cap with diamond pattern, with deep ribbed, ruffled cuff and top knot.

Sizes

To fit Petite/6 months (Small/1 year, Medium/2 years, Large/4 years)

Finished circumference:
14 (15.5, 16.5, 18)"
<35.5 (39.5, 42, 45.5) cm>

Ruffle and Cuff

With smaller dpn, cast on 160 (168, 184, 208) sts, dividing sts evenly over 3 needles. Join, taking care not to twist sts on needles and place marker for beg of rnd. Work in k4, p4 rib for ruffle. Next rnd: K0 (8, 8, 0), *k2 tog; rep from * around—80 (88, 96, 104) sts. Cont in k3, p1 rib for 2 (2, 2, 3)" <5 (5, 5, 7.5) cm>. P next rnd for turning ridge. Turn work and change to larger dpn. Next rnd (WS of rib, RS of body): Cont in chart pat until 8 rows of chart have been worked 5 (5, 6, 7) times. Next rnd: *K2 tog, p2 tog; rep from * around—40 (44, 48, 52) sts. Next rnd: *P2 tog, k2 tog; rep from * around—20 (22, 24, 26) sts. Cont in this way to alternate k2 tog and p2 tog (to form Seed st) until there are 6 sts. Work in St st (k every rnd) on these 6 sts for top knot for 3.5" <9cm>. Fasten off. Draw through sts, pull tog tightly and secure. Tie in a knot.

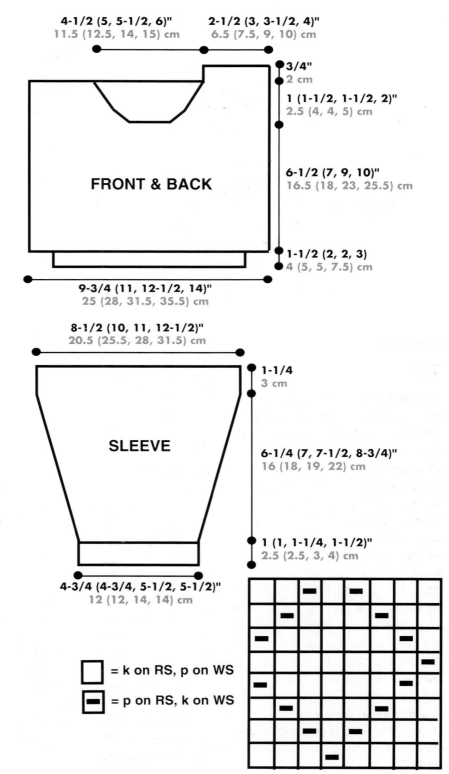

FRONT & BACK

4-1/2 (5, 5-1/2, 6)"
11.5 (12.5, 14, 15) cm

2-1/2 (3, 3-1/2, 4)"
6.5 (7.5, 9, 10) cm

3/4"
2 cm

1 (1-1/2, 1-1/2, 2)"
2.5 (4, 4, 5) cm

6-1/2 (7, 9, 10)"
16.5 (18, 23, 25.5) cm

1-1/2 (2, 2, 3)
4 (5, 5, 7.5) cm

9-3/4 (11, 12-1/2, 14)"
25 (28, 31.5, 35.5) cm

SLEEVE

8-1/2 (10, 11, 12-1/2)"
20.5 (25.5, 28, 31.5) cm

1-1/4
3 cm

6-1/4 (7, 7-1/2, 8-3/4)"
16 (18, 19, 22) cm

1 (1, 1-1/4, 1-1/2)"
2.5 (2.5, 3, 4) cm

4-3/4 (4-3/4, 5-1/2, 5-1/2)"
12 (12, 14, 14) cm

☐ = k on RS, p on WS

⊟ = p on RS, k on WS

Firecrackers

Sizes

To fit Small/3-6 months (Medium/1-2 years, Large/3-4 years)

Finished circumference: 16 (18.5, 20.5)" <40.5 (47, 52) cm>

Materials

Sport weight wool that will obtain gauge given below

45 (50, 100) yards <40 (45, 90) meters> each colors A, B, C, D, E, F, G and H

Knitting needles size 5 US (8 UK, 4mm) *or size needed to obtain gauge*. Size C (12 UK, 2.50mm) crochet hook.

Sample in photograph knit in Rowan Lightweight DK, #62 Black (A), #110 White (B), #25 Orange (C), #96 Cerise Red (D), #501 Purple (E), #32 Lt. Green (F), #90 Teal (G), #51 Blue (H)

Gauge

26 sts and 28 rows = 4" <10 cm> in Stockinette st and color-work patterns.

Always check gauge to save time and ensure correct yardage!

I couldn't resist including one wildly colored piece! This mini helmet with earflaps is small, so it knits up quickly. The double colors give you a hat that is doubly warm as well as witty, so give it a try, even if you usually avoid carrying colors! You use only two colors at a time, which simplifies the process.

Row 32: With H, (p 9 (10, 8), p2 tog) 9 (9, 12) times, to 90 (99, 108) sts. Row 33v Rep row 31. Row 34: *2H, 1C, 3H; rep from *. Row 35: Work 1 row H. Row 36: With H, (p3 (9, 10), p2 tog) 18 (9, 9) times, to 72 (90, 99) sts. Row 37: Rep row 35. Row 38: *1E, 1G; rep from *. Row 39: Match colors. Cont with D to end of hat, AT SAME TIME, *for size large only*, dec 9 sts evenly on next row, to 90 sts, then work 1 row even. *For all sizes*, cont to dec 18 sts evenly every other row until there are 18 sts. K2 tog across last RS row. Fasten off. Draw through sts, pull tog tightly and secure. Sew back seam.

Earflaps (make 2)

With A, cast on 1 st. Work in St st (k on RS, p on WS) and work incs and pats simultaneously as foll: Inc 1 st each side every row 11 (12, 13) times, AT SAME TIME, work pats as foll: Row 1: *1A, 1B; rep from *. Row 2: Work A sts with B and B sts with A. Rows 3 and 4: Work 2 rows A. Row 5: *1D, 1E; rep from *. Row 6: Work E sts with D and D sts with E. Rows 7 and 8: Work 2 rows E. Work rem of flap with A. Place 23 (25, 27) sts on a holder.

Hat

With A, cast on 14 (16, 18) sts for one half back, k across 23 (25, 27) sts of one earflap, cast on 34 (38, 42) sts for front, k across 23 (25, 27) sts of 2nd earflap, cast on 14 (16, 18) sts for 2nd half of back. Cont in pats on 108 (120, 132) sts as foll: Row 1 (RS): *3A, 3B; rep from *. Rows 2 and 3: Match colors. Row 4: Work A sts with B and B sts with A. Rows 5 and 6: Match colors. Rows 7 and 8: Work 2 rows C. Row 9: *1C, 1D; rep from *. Row 10: Work C sts with D and D sts with C. Row 11: Work 1 row D. Rows 12 and 13: Work 2 rows E. Rows 14-19: Work 6 rows chart pat. Rows 20 and 21: Work 2 rows E. Rows 22-27: Rep rows 1-6. Row 28: Work 1 row D. Row 29: *1D, 1F; rep from *. Row 30 (WS): With D, (p10 (8, 9), p2 tog) 9 (12, 12) times, to 99 (108, 120) sts. Row 31: Work 1 row H.

Finishing

With crochet hook and A, make two 7" <18cm> chains, and sew to end of flaps. Make 2 medium pom-poms, one with E and 1 with F and sew to end of ch. Make 1 large pom-pom with C and sew to top of hat.

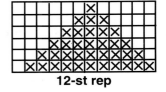

12-st rep

☐ = G

☒ = F

TIPS FOR KNITTERS: THE BASICS

Yarn Selection

The patterns in this book are generic. Although I've listed the actual yarns used for the samples shown in the photographs, you can substitute other yarns with perfect ease, according to availability and individual tastes.

To determine how much yarn you'll need, find the number of yards (or meters) on the ball band, then divide that figure into the number of yards (or meters) called for in the project. Always round up the final number. It's better to have a bit extra than to run out, since two dye lots of the "same" color can be quite different. (If you do run out, avoid an abrupt color change by alternating a row of the old yarn with a row of the new one for several rows.)

Use the very best yarns you can afford, in natural fibers and blends. There are many good superwash wools and washable, durable cottons on the market now, all easily available. If you're going to spend hours building a garment, shouldn't you have only the most beautiful yarns in your hands? After all, you just might be creating an heirloom!

Gauge

I can't say enough about gauge! A gauge swatch—a small, easy-to-knit, 4-inch (10 cm) square of knitting—will make all the difference in the success of your project. Many knitters want to begin the garment right away, using the recommended needles and yarn, but making a gauge swatch first is critically important. No matter how beautifully you knit, if your gauge is off, your garment will end up too large or too small. When you get the exact gauge, your garment will always fit perfectly.

Never assume your gauge is the same as indicated on the yarn label; differences in each individual knitter's tension and speed, plus different needles and yarns, add up to essentially different measurements. Please, just do it! You will see remarkable results in your work.

I always save my gauge swatches, along with a few yards of the original yarn and notes about the project, for future research or mending if necessary. Saving these items along with the patterns makes a delightful knitting history if kept in a loose-leaf binder.

How to Make a Gauge Swatch

Using the recommended needles and yarn and the basic gauge noted in the pattern, cast on enough stitches to make a 4" <10cm> square swatch, plus 6 sts. Work 3 rows of garter st, k every row. Next row, begin your pattern st, always working 3 sts each end in garter st. Continue until pattern work measures 4" <10cm>, work 3 more rows garter, and bind off. Stretch your swatch gently from all sides, and place on a flat surface. If your swatch does not measure 4" <10cm> across, change to needles one size larger or smaller, as need be, until you get an exact measurement. Being even half a stitch off gauge can result in a garment that is much too big or too small. For example, if the gauge is 5 sts = 1" <2.5cm> and you are actually getting 4.5 sts, then on a size 2, 22" <56cm> sweater you will be 10 sts, or 2" <5cm>, larger in circumference on your finished size—quite a difference on any garment!

If you have too few stitches per inch (or centimeter), your tension is too loose; change to a smaller size needle to compensate. If you have too many stitches, go up to a larger size needle to correct tension that is too tight.

All ribbing should be firmly knit; change to a smaller needle if your knitting tends to be loose. You may also want to add an invisible elastic yarn to ribbing, to prevent sagging or stretching.

Row Counting

If you count your rows, garment pieces will always match perfectly, for easy finishing and splendid results. I usually lace a yarn of a different color up the front of the work, catching it in every 5 or 10 rows, for easy counting. These measuring strands can be left in until the very end, which makes fitting and measuring a snap.

Sizing

It is important to choose the correct size for your project. I use a larger template than is usually found in American pattern design, so extra attention is wise. If possible, measure the child loosely under the arms; chest size is often the key to correct fit. You might also measure a garment that fits the child very well and compare it to these measurements.

You might also want to consider growth rate, since your goal is a garment that will fit when it's finished, not when it's begun. While these patterns knit up quickly, children grow in a flash. Allowing some extra room for growth is always a good idea. It's better to have a garment that's too big than one that's too small; no child is going to shrink into a sweater!

You can alter most patterns easily to fit a specific child, adjusting sleeve length, shoulder to waist length, or pant length in the body of the piece. (Make your adjustments in the lower section of the sleeve or pant leg.) Make sure to adjust the pattern as well when altering, working it out on graph paper before you knit!

Several sizes are included for each design. The smallest size is given first, with increasingly larger sizes given in parentheses. If you want to make a size Large, and the sizes given are Small (Medium, Large), always work the last set of numbers in the parentheses.

Colorwork

Adding a second or third color gives a garment a dashing look. Most of the colorwork in these projects consists of simply changing from one color yarn to another as you change rows. On

some, however, two colors are used together in the same row. I try to reserve two-color knitting for details, edging, or accents, which adds a lot of color with a minimum of work. Working with two colors at once is easier than it might appear at first. Give it a try; I think you'll be delighted with your results!

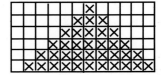

Sample Color Chart

Color charts are included for projects that involve stranded two-color knitting. A color chart indicates the placement of colors on the right side of the fabric and is usually read from right to left, beginning at the lower right. Each square of the chart indicates one stitch, building in rows from the bottom up.

Jacquard is the general term for any stranded two-color knitting. It can be worked two ways: by the *Fair Isle* method or by *intarsia*. True Fair Isle knitting is done in the round, but will work on two needles as well if you prefer. It's often used for geometric designs (such as diamonds), snowflakes, and overall dot patterns. Intarsia is used for large areas of color that extend vertically as well as horizontally.

Fair Isle

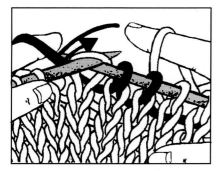

Knitting with the right hand, stranding with the left

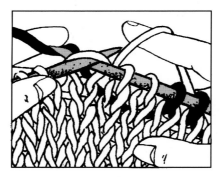

Purling with the left hand, stranding with the right

Purling with the right hand, stranding with the left

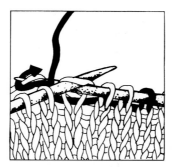

Weaving yarns when changing colors on knit rows

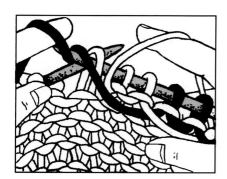

Knitting with the left hand, stranding with the right

In Fair Isle knitting, the color not being knitted is carried, or *stranded*, behind the work. It's easy to do. Work one or two stitches in color A, then weave color B—the yarn being stranded—*over* color A. Work one or two more stitches in color A, then weave color B *under* color A. Continue in this way until it's time to change colors—to knit with color B and strand color A.

I never carry yarn across more than three stitches at a time. A long carry-over, or *float*, often pulls the fabric, ruins the tension, and makes a fabric that is easily snagged—not good for children's wear. This technique will make a big difference in the quality of your two-color work. At the edge of the row, carry unused colors easily up the edges, catching it in every few rows to avoid pulling.

The most difficult (and perhaps daunting) aspect of Fair Isle knitting is maintaining an even tension. Yarns should be carried loosely across the back of the work. It will help to constantly spread the stitches out after they are knit to insure that enough yarn has been carried to stretch across the back without pulling.

Intarsia

To knit with the intarsia technique, wind each color yarn onto a bobbin. (Commercial bobbins are available at yarn shops.) Working with the first color, knit the number of stitches specified in the chart. To join the second color yarn, twist the second color around the stitch just knit and continue knitting with the second color. Continue twisting the yarns around each

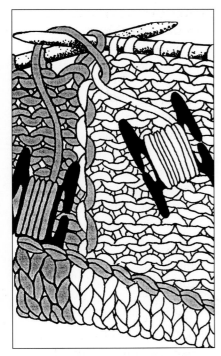

Using bobbins for intarsia knitting

other every row to form a joint at each color change, creating a single layer of fabric and preventing holes.

Blocking

Blocking doesn't take long and it improves the look of your finished garment. After completing the knitting and weaving in all yarn tails, cover the garment pieces with two terry cloth towels, leaving the ribbed areas uncovered. Steam lightly at the appropriate temperature setting for the yarn you have used. Let the pieces dry flat for perfect results.

Finishing

Always do your finishing in the morning, in good light, on a flat surface. This may sound self-evident, but I learned it the hard way! In the excitement of finally completing the knitting, it's tempting to go ahead and finish the garment, even if it's midnight. Beautiful finishing makes an incredible difference, so it's worth waiting until you're fresh.

Laundering

You can use your original gauge swatch for a washability test, following the instructions on the yarn band. Laundering machine washables in a mesh bag keeps them from being stretched out of shape. Dry the garments flat, then gently pull them into their original shapes.

Abbreviations

beg	beginning
cont	continue
dec	decrease
foll	follows
inc	increase
k	knit
p	purl
psso	pass slipped stitch over
rep	repeat
rev	reverse Stockinette stitch
RS	right side
sc	single chain
skp	slip one, knit one, PSSO
sl	slip
sl st	slip stitch
ssk	slip, slip, knit
St st	Stockinette stitch
tbl	through back loop
tog	together
WS	wrong side
wyib	with yarn in back
wyif	with yarn in front
yo	yarn over

ACKNOWLEDGEMENTS

Carla Patrick, my technical editor, has been absolutely invaluable, translating my original patterns into American Knitting Language. Her meticulous skills, talents, and good nature are boundless.

Since the beginning, Minnowknits photography has been done by Nina Fuller Carter, with whom I have shared everything from studios to bringing up children over many years. Her work is sensitive, perceptive, and clear of vision. It is never easy to coax a baby into the perfect shot, but children blossom under the gaze of her lens and the warmth of her inimitable charm.

Several gifted stylists have contributed their eagle eyes to our photo shoots, including Chris Cantwell and Isabel Smiles in the studio, and, most intensively, Merle Hagelin, both in the studio and on location. "Baby wrangling," as it is known in the trade, is the most difficult of a stylist's endeavors, given that most babies are put on set only to scamper quickly off like a well-wound windup toy, crawling out of focus or out of costume with astonishing speed. Hats come flying off heads and glee quickly turns to tears, so our photo shoots are brisk, spirited, and tinged with a bit of luck. Merle has ample opportunity to show off her many talents!

My band of wonderful knitters for this collection includes Ann Baldwin, Connie Gemmer, Mary Milam, Mary Merrill, Jane Howard, Isabel Smiles, and Nita Young. Faced with a demanding production schedule, their nimble fingers flew for weeks, producing all the hand-knitted garments. Knitting prototype patterns for the first time—on deadline for photography to boot—requires expert knitting skills and a learned eye. Pattern checking, a difficult but oh-so-important task, was meticulously accomplished by our master knitter, Mary Milam.

Our location photography was shot in and around the Pomegranate Inn in Portland, Maine, thanks to the generosity of Alan and Isabel Smiles.

Merci

I would like to thank my husband, David Nichols Eaton, for his unbelievable support throughout my wild and woolly design career. Connie Gemmer, a wonderful friend and gifted knitter, got me back to knitting after a hiatus of busy knitless years and encouraged me to publish my pattern line from the very beginning. My dear friend Isabel Smiles has such a talented design sense that when she encouraged me to begin my knitting design business, I believed I could do it! Sarah Minton, a knitting master, taught me exquisite finishing techniques and the art of the detail, and always promoted my designs. Thanks to Jody Halliday, owner of the Martha Hall Natural Fibres shop in Yarmouth, Maine, for taking my first pattern on first sight and publishing it in her national mail-order catalogue, and to Penelope Coit for unlimited friendship and support, reading drafts, and design applause.

Big thanks to my literary agent, Sandra Taylor, and my publisher, Rob Pulleyn, for believing in my ideas and for taking a chance on the new kid on the block.

And last, but certainly not least, I want to thank my business partner, Cos Lattanzi, for her extraordinary work, aesthetic point of view, enormous understanding, clear thinking under fire, multifaceted talents, boundless energy, and contagious laughter.

MODELS

Special thanks go to our adorable models, whose spirit and charm always bring the clothes to life!

They came from all the expected places—kids of friends and staff members, associates' nieces, nephews, and grandchildren. But some were discovered in supermarket baskets and doctor's offices, and one from the middle of a nursery school parade! One delightful find, Noel Surprise, came through Portland Models Group; at the last minute, our scheduled model canceled and we needed an emergency replacement for the Surprise! Chapeau (angels at work, no doubt).

Introduction Mary Elizabeth Badger &
Bennet Lusk Brainard

Bambinis
Chapter opener   Emily Gibson and
Zack the Dog
Baby Brit Sailor   Matthew Wilson
Tangerina   Chloe Kubo & Sasha Timson
Bon Bons   Bennett Lusk Brainard &
Jordan and Janelle Lyford
Zany Bambini   Farr Bryant
Beau Jest   Katherine Whitaker

Jumping Beans
Chapter opener   Lorenza Sophia Lattanzi
Polka Dots   Sarah Ayers
Gumdrops   Hannah Milam
Coco Chenille   Mary Elizabeth Badger
Parfait   Brianna Lindsay
Yikes! Stripes!   Lily Fuller Hoffman
Tennis, Anyone?   Matthew Ayers

Holidays
Chapter opener   Eleanor McKinney & Erika Joyce
Holiday Dress   Noel Surprise
Party Dress   Mary Fagin
Petite Chic   Sasha Timpson
La Pinafore   Tara Milliken & Halsey Leighton
Brit Jacket   Alexander Arbuckle
Buttons & Bows   Tara Milliken

Great Outdoors
Chapter opener   Annie & Louisa Gemmer &
Spencer Hoffman
Red Riding Hood   Lorenza Sophia Lattanzi
Surprise Chapeau Noel Surprise
Aran Ruffles   Farr Bryant
Ski, Baby!   Brice Farnum
Skating   Kacy Barton
Faux Fisherman   Cary Gemmer &
Alexander Lord Eaton
Firecrackers   Erika Joyce

SUPPLIERS

While the patterns in this book are generic—the gauge, rather than an exact yarn, is specified—we do identify the yarns used for the sample garments modeled in the photographs. The companies listed below sell these yarns (some of the best available on the market) and can tell you where to find them in your area.

Australia
Rowan Yarns
Sunspun Enterprises Pty Ltd.
195 Canterbury Road
Canterbury, 3126 Victoria

Canada
S.R. Kertzer
105A Winges Road
Woodbridge, Ontario L4L 6C2

New Zealand
Alliance Knitting Yarns
Factory Road
Mosgiel

United Kingdom
Rowan Yarns
Green Lane Mill
Washpit, Holmfirth
West Yorkshire HD7 1RW

USA
Classic Elite Yarns
12 Perkins St.
Lowell, MA 10854

Crystal Palace Yarns
3006 San Pablo Avenue
Berkeley, CA 94702

Cynthia Helene Yarns
Unique Kolours
8 East Main Street
Moorestown, NJ 08057

Manos Distributors USA
Simpson Southwick
RR2, Box 468, Rte 513
Califon, NJ 07830

Rowan Yarns
Westminster Trading Corporation
5 Northern Boulevard
Amherst, NH 03031

BIBLIOGRAPHY

Bredewold, Ank, and Anneke Pleiter. *The Knitting Design Book.* Asheville, NC: Lark Books, 1988.

Hiatt, June Hemmons. *The Principles of Knitting.* New York: Simon and Schuster, 1988.

Goldberg, Rhoda Ochser. *The New Knitting Dictionary.* New York: Crown Publishers, 1984.

Editors of Vogue Knitting. *Vogue Knitting Book.* New York: Pantheon Books, 1989.

Norbury, James, and Margaret Agutter. *Odhams Encyclopedia of Knitting.* London: Odhams Books Ltd., 1957.

Stanley, Montse. *The Handknitter's Handbook.* London: David and Charles, 1986.

Thomas, Mary. *Mary Thomas's Book of Knitting Patterns.* London: Hodder and Stoughton, Ltd., 1943. Reprint. New York: Dover Publications, Inc., 1972.

Zimmerman, Elizabeth. *Knitter's Almanac.* New York: Charles Scribner's Sons, 1974. Reprint, New York: Dover Publications, Inc., 1981.

———. *Knitting Without Tears.* New York: Charles Scribner's Sons, 1971.

INDEX

Instructions for this romper are found on page 16.